THE POLISH PEASANT IN EUROPE AND AMERICA

A Classic Work in Immigration History

THE
POLISH PEASANT
IN EUROPE
AND AMERICA

*A Classic Work
in Immigration History*

WILLIAM I. THOMAS
AND
FLORIAN ZNANIECKI

Edited by Eli Zaretsky

UNIVERSITY OF ILLINOIS PRESS
Urbana and Chicago

This book is printed on acid-free paper.

Library of Congress Cataloging-in-Publication Data

Thomas, William Isaac, 1863–1947.
   The Polish peasant in Europe and America : a classic work in
immigration history / William I. Thomas and Florian Znaniecki ;
edited by Eli Zaretsky.
      p.   cm.
   ISBN 0-252-06484-4 (pbk.)
   1. Polish Americans—Social conditions. 2. Peasantry—Poland.
3. Poland—Social conditions. I. Znaniecki, Florian, 1882–1958.
II. Zaretsky, Eli. III. Title.
E184.P7T48   1996
305.891'85073—dc20   95-838
                                                      CIP

Digitally reprinted from the first paperback printing

To the memory of my father,
David Zaretsky,
1907–93

CONTENTS

INTRODUCTION

Eli Zaretsky

During the past generation, the understanding of American history has been revolutionized by the development of a new school of historical thought—social history. Whereas earlier historians focused on the higher reaches of power—politics, war, high culture—social historians attempted to see history as a scene of conflict. Some social historians sought to write history "from the bottom up," in other words, to understand the shape that the struggles of ordinary men and women—slaves, peasants, workers—gave to history. Others emphasized the ways in which class relations, for example, between slave and master or capitalist and worker, shaped history. In either case social historians were concerned to recast history to bring out the role of ordinary men and women.

This was not the first time that scholars had made such an attempt. During the Progressive Era, the period between the late 1890s and World War I, American reformers and intellectuals also sought to understand the rapidly changing American working class and the urban and immigrant poor. Their work took such forms as journalistic exposés and "muckraking," government surveys and studies, novels and immigrant biographies. Among its most significant expressions was a new university discipline, sociology. William I. Thomas and Florian Znaniecki's *Polish Peasant in Europe and America,* published in five volumes between 1918 and 1920, is the founding work of that discipline. It shaped American thought as well as social policy until late into the twentieth century.

During the Progressive Era, immigration posed a major problem for many native-born Americans. For one thing, the number of immigrants who came to America in this period was enormous: in many cities a majority of the population were either immigrants or the children of immigrants. Some native-born Americans felt that the cultural, religious, and racial identity of their country was threatened. The immigrants were in large part industrial workers and thus were linked in the popular mind with unionization and radicalism. Because many of them were poor, they were associated with crime and social breakdown, especially the breakdown of the family. Because they relied on political parties to help them find jobs, housing, and, when necessary, relief, some progressives associated immigration with political corruption.

The Polish Peasant in Europe and America was one of the earliest works to study the culture and social organization of immigrants. Not only did Thomas and Znaniecki appreciate the potential contribution of the immigrants to American culture, but they also tried to understand the immigrants' culture in its own terms. This effort had two dimensions. First, Thomas and Znaniecki invented what was at that point a new method of social investigation—the life study method. The essence of this method was in getting the immigrants to tell their own life stories, either by hiring them to do so or by finding documents, especially letters, in which they did. In addition, *The Polish Peasant* inaugurated the first truly transatlantic approach to European emigration, one that looked at both its European and its United States context. This approach relates *The Polish Peasant* to recent developments among social historians such as Josef Barton, Kerby Miller, and, on Poland, John Bukowczyk.[1]

William I. Thomas, the principal author of the work, was typical of the first generation of American sociologists. He was born in 1863; his background was rural (Virginia and Tennessee) and religious (Methodist); he was originally trained in another discipline (literature), studied in Germany, and came to Chicago in 1893 to earn a second doctorate in sociology. The University of Chicago had the leading—practically the only—sociology department in the nation. Almost as important to Thomas as the university was Hull-House, the most famous settlement house in America, where he lectured and dined. Thomas was a sophisticated, worldly, friendly man; he liked good clothing, he enjoyed golf, and he moved easily in different currents of society. He was politically active in such causes as woman suffrage, prostitution reform, and the advancement of civil liberties.

Thomas came to write *The Polish Peasant* after the success of his first book, *Sex and Society* (1907), an anthropological explanation of the causes of women's oppression. Helen Culver, a philanthropist of the time and heir to the fortune that had endowed Hull-

House, was impressed with the book and donated $50,000 so that Thomas could "study an immigrant group in Europe and America to determine as far as possible what relation their home mores and norms had to their adjustment and maladjustment in America."[2] *The Polish Peasant* is dedicated to Culver.

In spite of his worldliness, Thomas saw himself as an immigrant. In a brief 1928 autobiographical statement he wrote: "I was born in an isolated region of Old Virginia, 20 miles from the railroad in a social environment resembling that of the 18th century, and I consequently feel that I have lived in three centuries, migrating gradually toward the higher cultural areas."[3] Thomas believed that the experience of moving from a traditional and rural culture to a modern and urban one was, in essence, universal. A young man or woman leaving a farm in rural America to find an urban job, an African American leaving the rural South to move to Harlem or Chicago, a young Pole moving to Pittsburgh to work in a steel mill, an Italian family emigrating to work in a Buffalo cannery— in all these cases, the individual was leaving behind a close-knit, family-based, traditional culture and seeking to adapt to a more individualistic and competitive world.

Thomas's first plan was to compare immigration from the South, the West Indies, and West Africa.[4] In 1913, however, he met Florian Znaniecki, a philosopher nineteen years his junior, who was working with emigrants in Warsaw (having been prevented from teaching because of his activities in favor of Polish independence). The next year Znaniecki came to Chicago to work as Thomas's translator and convinced Thomas to study only Polish immigrants. After Znaniecki wrote a long methodological statement with which the original work began, the men agreed on joint authorship.[5]

Thomas and Znaniecki's subject was the approximately two million Poles who immigrated to America between 1880 and 1910. During the Napoleonic wars, Poland had been partitioned among Austria, Prussia, and Russia. *The Polish Peasant* is primarily concerned with Russian, or Congress, Poland, from which mostly single, young male laborers emigrated. Probably a different story would have been told had Thomas and Znaniecki studied Austrian or Prussian Poland, from which entire family units tended to emigrate.

For centuries agriculture in Congress Poland had been divided between manors, tilled by compulsory peasant labor, and village land held in common. In 1864 a peasant insurrection occurred, roughly contemporary with the abolition of slavery in the United States. In response, the Russians abolished compulsory labor, indemnified the nobles, and divided the common land among the peasants. These acts created a landowning peasantry and opened the countryside to commercial competition. The development of railways and steamships further integrated Polish agriculture into the world economy and left the countryside vulnerable to international economic swings. The generation of peasants studied by Thomas and Znaniecki was the first to experience a full-fledged monetary economy, with its accompanying population pressures, and division and concentration of land.[6]

By the time the Poles began emigrating, Congress Poland had become a center of Russian industrial development. Warsaw was the major point of exchange on the state railway system that linked Russia to the West. Lodz, the center of the Polish textile industry, was one of the most rapidly industrializing cities in the world. The demand for labor in these cities as well as the availability of better-paying agricultural employment in Germany and Denmark occurred at the same time as instability and competition pushed a surplus population out of the countryside. One historian has described the Slavic emigrants of this period as part of "a peasant proletariat, roaming the countryside, indeed the world, in search of employment in agriculture and industry."[7] An important contribution of *The Polish Peasant* is in refuting the stereotype of preindustrial peasants arriving suddenly in New York; most Polish immigrants to America had previously emigrated to other cities in Europe.

Before *The Polish Peasant*, immigrants were mostly studied through "social surveys" that amassed data without analyzing causes. Thomas and Znaniecki called this "common-sense sociology." The general approach tended to be moralistic and to blame the poor. For example, *The Pittsburgh Survey* stated: "Do you wish to catch glimpses of the problem of recreation? . . . You need only happen in at the Hollow, and see how disintegrating forces assert themselves, when the progressive ones are shut off through civil lethargy and selfishness."[8] Thomas and Znaniecki, by contrast, sought to explain social problems by examining the relation between individuals and their surrounding society. The key unit to look at, they argued, was not government but family, neighborhood, and other community ties. One reason they were interested in Poland is that, because it was occupied by foreign powers, reform activity was at the local level. In the context of early twentieth-century America, Thomas and Znaniecki opposed laissez-faire conservatives who believed that everything was up to the individual as well as progressives who thought government could manage social problems. Groups, not individuals nor state technocrats, they argued, were the key to social change.

To support this argument Thomas and Znaniecki tried to show that the Poles were held together primarily by *social* ties. In traditional Poland, people were motivated by a felt wish for face-to-face response from others and also by a wish for recognition in the eyes of the community. Only very slowly did Polish peasants learn to think economically, in other words, to think in terms of bargaining, exchange, and the advantages to be gained from others. Thomas and Znaniecki's main concern was to analyze the process by which peasants turned into economically rational workers and citizens, both in Poland and, after emigrating, in the United States. In doing so they stressed that individuals changed by adapting to social groups to which they were connected, groups that were themselves changing. The most important group was the family, by which Thomas and Znaniecki meant extended relations rather than the nuclear family alone.

The stress on the group runs through *The Polish Peasant*. First, Thomas and Znaniecki show that social intimidation holds together the old society even when it no longer serves people's needs. When people change—when they modernize their agriculture, begin to consider women's rights, learn to read, or try to stop smoking—they do so with the help of others. When they emigrate, they emigrate as groups, not as individuals, and they retain their connections to their native land. When social breakdown—crime, wife beating, economic demoralization—does occur, Thomas and Znaniecki claim, it is because individuals have become isolated. When American social work functions badly, it is because it works with individuals and does not draw on the strengths of the group. Finally, they established that the Poles and other immigrants have something special to contribute to America, namely, their group feeling, which is a more important contribution, according to Thomas and Znaniecki, than native costumes or music.

In 1918, soon after the publication of the first two volumes of *The Polish Peasant*, Thomas was arrested by agents of the Federal Bureau of Investigation and charged with violating the Mann Act by transporting women across state lines for immoral purposes. (What brought Thomas to the FBI's attention was probably the antiwar activity of his wife.) The University of Chicago fired him and stopped publication of the book; the last three volumes were published in Boston by an obscure press. Thomas never again held a regular university position, and Znaniecki returned to teach in Poland until the 1930s.[9] The arrest detracted from immediate acknowledgment of the book's significance. Nonetheless, *The Polish Peasant* was the most important influence on American social scientists and social workers for many decades.

The generation of sociologists inspired by *The Polish Peasant* was called the "Chicago school." They not only taught at the University of Chicago, they also used the city's stockyards, labor movement, and immigrant neighborhoods as a sociological laboratory. In contrast to the idea that the immigrants should be Americanized, the Chicago school explained the importance of the city's ethnic colonies and neighborhoods in protecting the immigrants. The unmarried Persian men whose life centered on the coffeehouse and steamship agency, the Greek lodging houses, the family-centered Sicilian neighborhoods—these and other neighborhoods created the mosaic of immigrant life. In communities, wrote one sociologist, the immigrant finds "a social world . . . has status, plays a role in a group . . . finds response and security."[10] The Chicago sociologists extended Thomas and Znaniecki's analysis to blacks and Asians. For example, E. Franklin Frazier explained desertion and divorce in the Northern black family as the consequence of the impact of urban life on family organization and folk culture developed in the rural South.[11]

By World War II, the influence of *The Polish Peasant* declined as social scientists turned increasingly toward European social theory and quantitative studies. At the same time, the book became newly influential among the historians who wrote the first histories of U.S. immigration. The most important of these historians was Oscar Handlin, who took the Chicago studies of ethnicity as his model for *Boston's Immigrants* and took *The Polish Peasant* as his model for his enormously influential synthesis of the immigrant experience, *The Uprooted*.[12]

In *The Uprooted*, Handlin did not look at differences between immigrant groups; rather he tried to understand the experience of the typical immigrant. Following the precedent of *The Polish Peasant*, he showed how immigrants used their traditional culture to come to terms with American conditions: "The man who joined a mutual aid association was adjusting thereby to the environment of the United States," not merely preserving his traditional culture. For Handlin, the point of this adjustment was individual freedom and mobility, which made the immigrant typically American. America, Handlin wrote, "is the land of separated men."[13]

The social histories, including African-American history, labor history, and women's history, written in the 1960s were originally directed in part against Handlin's work. For Handlin, and even for the Chicago school of sociologists, ethnicity conditioned entry into a predominantly individualistic, upwardly striving nation. By contrast, Herbert Gutman, the most important of the early American social historians, showed that ethnicity could serve as a point of resistance to, or at most a grudging acceptance of, a class society.[14] The difference in Gutman's account suggested the possibility of an entirely new way of viewing modern American history. Historians since Gutman have established the place of the Polish immigrants in American working class history, a perspective strikingly missing from Thomas and Znaniecki's perspective. In an epilogue to this work, I summarize our contemporary understanding of the Polish immigration as social historians have conceptualized it.

*   *   *

I have broken the selections that follow into four parts: the Polish background; the peasant letters, which record the changes in family life that accompanied immigration; the social disorganization in the United States that sometimes accompanied immigration; and the discovery of ethnicity and the ethnic community in the United States. Source lines provided at the beginning of each section refer to the volume and pages of the original five-volume edition from which the selections in this classroom edition were taken. The subdivisions in part 4 were added by me.

NOTES

1. Josef Barton, *Peasants and Strangers: Italians, Rumanians, and Slovaks in an American City, 1890–1950* (Cambridge: Harvard University Press, 1975); Kerby Miller, *Emigrants and Exiles* (New York: Oxford University Press, 1985); John Bukowczyk, *And My Children Did Not Know Me: A History of the Polish-Americans* (Bloomington: Indiana University Press, 1987).

2. Thomas quoted in Herbert Blumer, *An Appraisal of Thomas and Znaniecki's "The Polish Peasant in Europe and America"* (New York: Social Science Research Council, 1939), p. 103.

3. William Isaac Thomas, "My Life" (1928), quoted in Carla Cappetti, "Deviant Girls and Dissatisfied Women: A Sociologist's Tale," in *The Invention of Ethnicity*, ed. Werner Sollors (New York: Oxford University Press, 1989), p. 124.

4. Cappetti, p. 104. See also Thomas to Robert E. Park, Apr. 23, 1912, Robert E. Park Collection, University of Chicago Library. Thomas left no papers.

5. See Morris Janowitz, "Introduction" in *William I. Thomas on Social Organization and Social Personality, Selected Papers*, ed. Morris Janowitz (Chicago: Phoenix Books, 1966), pp. xxiii–xxviii; Robert Bierstedt, *Florian Znaniecki on Humanistic Sociology* (Chicago: University of Chicago Press, 1969), pp. 1–15; Florian Znaniecki, "William I. Thomas as a Collaborator," *Sociology and Social Research* 32 (1948): 765–67; Winifred Rauschenbush, *Robert E. Park: Biography of a Sociologist* (Durham: Duke University Press, 1979), pp. 67–76.

6. See Stefan Kieniewicz, *The Emancipation of the Polish Peasantry* (Chicago: University of Chicago Press, 1969), p. 4; J. Rose, "Russian Poland in the Later Nineteenth Century," in *The Cambridge History of Poland, 1697–1935*, F. Reddaway et al. (New York: Octagon Books, 1971).

7. Victor Greene, *The Slavic Community on Strike* (Notre Dame: Notre Dame University Press, 1968), p. 26. See also Caroline Golab, "The Polish Experience in Philadelphia," in *The Ethnic Experience in Pennsylvania*, ed. John Bodnar (Lewisburg, Pa.: Bucknell University Press, 1973), pp. 39–73; and Golab, *Immigrant Destinations* (Philadelphia: Temple University Press, 1977), pp. 48–49, 93–94.

8. Florence Lattimore, "Three Studies in Housing and Responsibility," in *The Pittsburgh Survey*, ed. Paul Kellog (New York: Survey Associates, Russell Sage Foundation, 1914), 5:124, 6:351. My discussion draws from David Matza, *Becoming Deviant* (Englewood Cliffs, N.J.: Prentice-Hall, 1969), pp. 17–24.

9. On Thomas's Mann Act arrest see Znaniecki, "William I. Thomas as a Collaborator," pp. 765–67; and Raushnenbush, *Robert E. Park*, pp. 67–76.

10. Harvey Warren Zorbaugh, *The Gold Coast and the Slum* (Chicago: University of Chicago Press, 1929), pp. 128, 134, 140–52.

11. E. Franklin Frazier, *Negro Family in the United States*, rev. and abr. ed. (Chicago: University of Chicago Press, 1966), p. 341.

12. Oscar Handlin, *Boston's Immigrants, 1790–1880: A Study in Acculturation* (rpt. 1958; Cambridge: Harvard University Press, 1941), and *The Uprooted: The Epic Story of the Great Migrations That Made the American People* (Boston: Little, Brown, 1951).

13. Handlin, *Uprooted,* pp. 5–6, 139–40, 152, 164–66, 175, 271–72. On Handlin see Maldwyn A. Jones, "Oscar Handlin," in *Pastmasters: Some Essays on American Historians,* ed. Marcus Cunliffe and Robin Winks (New York: Harper and Row, 1969), pp. 245–60.

14. Herbert G. Gutman, *Work, Culture, and Society* (New York: Knopf, 1976), p. 41.

THE POLISH PEASANT IN EUROPE AND AMERICA
A Classic Work in Immigration History

PART
1
THE POLISH BACKGROUND

In the first selection, a Polish priest explains how he uses the power of the Catholic confessional to shape his parishioners' attitudes. He counsels respect for authority and for private property, as well as providing advice concerning sexuality and marital practices.

Thomas and Znaniecki regard the priest as a kind of unthinking conservative who simply wants to preserve the old system, even though it no longer corresponds to popular attitudes and wishes. To contrast with the priest's unthinking rigidity, they present a series of letters to the editor of local self-help newspapers, aimed at fostering change. The point of the letters was to illustrate the importance of the community in the process of change. The newspapers were concerned with practical matters such as farming, gardening, and housekeeping; they also served as the vehicle of the nationalist awakening then sweeping through the Polish countryside. The letters express the importance of learning how to read, the importance of education, the importance of campaigning against drinking and smoking, and the importance of women's organizations in fostering social change. Thomas and Znaniecki's focus is on the interplay between individual change and the support the individual receives from the community. There were many parallels between these movements in Poland and the temperance, school reform, and women's organization movements in Progressive Era America.

THE PRIEST'S "CONFESSION"

The Catholic confession, according to the intention of the Church, is not only a disclosure of sins for the sake of remittance, but also a means of directing the believers, regulating their everyday life according to the Christian principles as they are exposed by the Catholic Church. . . . The activity of the confessor concerns: *sensual life*, *family [and community] life* (relation of husband and wife, education of children), [relation between members of the large family and the community], *economic life* (questions of expenses, wages paid to servants, conditions of work, etc.), *social life* (life in the state—question of taxes, of fulfilling duties; class relations; relation to Jews, etc.), *national life* (Polish language, national feeling, relation to national enemies), *church life* (fulfilling religious duties). . . .

Sensual life. Sexual questions are indubitably those most frequently raised during confession. . . . The regulation of sexual relations between husband and wife is a field of enormous influence of the priest. . . . The problem of avoiding a new increase of the family steps more and more frequently over the peasants' thresholds. And the priest must more and more frequently answer the questions of women, more scrupulous than men, whether washing the vagina after the coitus or using medicines is a sin or not. He must teach that conjugal onanism, use of pills, condoms, washing of the vagina are immoral, sinful, contrary to nature. In more serious cases, he must teach further what can be done with pure conscience (have relations only at a determined time).

Let us take some examples (I take them here merely from the standpoint of the church).

1. A woman complains that children emaciate her and that a physician told her that one more childbirth will kill her. But the husband does not even want to listen about stopping the sexual relation and orders her to take some pills into the vagina before the coitus. She had doubts for a long time and finally went to the priest for advice. . . . she does not want to die, but she neither can

---

4:103–20.

nor will refuse her husband, The priest stands before an alterna-
tive. If he says that it is a sin, the woman in spite of all will continue
to act in this way, and if he says that it is not a sin, he will act against
the moral law and his duties.

First of all, the priest should question the decision of the physician and send her to another. . . . Then—whether her husband
considers it sinless. If he does, then the priest must tell the woman
not to touch this question with her husband from the moral viewpoint, but to try to influence him so as to make him perform their
relation in a natural way. . . . Then he must tell the woman to re-
ject all fears, to try to strengthen herself as much as possible, and
to have the conjugal relation only at the time when the possibility
of fecundation is the smallest (that is, during the period of 10–14
days between one menstruation and another, avoiding sexual relation a week before and a week after the menses), although even this
is not an absolute security.[1] . . . The result is a normal life of husband and wife and more children. The physicians exaggerate very
frequently or follow the wish of the woman in their decisions. The
influence of religion, the belief in Providence often plays a great
role in dispelling the fear of childbirth. . . .

Sometimes the man has scruples as to whether he can have relations during pregnancy. Particularly among the peasants there is a
very strong sexual respect for a pregnant woman. The priest must
teach him that it is better to abstain, particularly during the first two
months, but if for the man there is *periculum incontinentiæ* he can,
but carefully. . . .

Very frequently people come with questions concerning the
quantity of sexual life. How often, whether it is a sin to do it while
completely nude; whether certain kisses and touches are a sin and
when. The rule is that between husband and wife some sexual abuses (lack of continence) can be only a venial sin if . . . the possibility
of fecundation is not excluded. . . .

System of treatment of sexual deviations. . . . As far as my personal
experience in the confessional has taught me, masturbation is a very
rare kind of sexual deviation among peasants, particularly in the
country. In towns it happens more frequently. . . . There is a great-

---

1. Note that the priest's advice is wrong: he is urging sexual intercourse at the
time when the possibility of fecundation is highest—ed.

er tendency to a normal satisfaction of the sexual instinct, particularly among boys, or to bestialism. The sexual intercourse of animals is usually a stimulus to analogous plays of boys in the period of puberty with girls below ten years of age. These offences are habitual in the poorer class of peasants, daily workers, servants, shepherds (mainly), youth as well as older people. Bestialism is relatively rather frequent among the country population. . . . Bestialism happens more frequently in the period of puberty (2 percent–3 percent) and then again toward the end of sexual life (1 percent) than in the period of maturity and happens almost exclusively among men, very seldom among women. . . . Pederasty is very rare among our peasants; it happens almost only among young people of small towns and only in the form of experiments. At least I have never observed it as a habitual vice. Relatively more frequent is Lesbian love among girls, but also only in towns and between servants living together. This manifestation is connected very frequently with a false devotion . . . and limits itself to very unelaborate means.

Intentional abortion . . . happens more frequently in towns than in villages. As far as I was able to observe the causes of this difference, these are: a greater dissoluteness, a looser idea of morality, the question of supporting children, which is more difficult in a town, and finally a greater facility for concealing the offense. . . . Abortion in towns happens more frequently among married women, in the country among girls. . . . On the other hand, there are in the country many vain endeavors to provoke abortion, such as charms, medicines, etc.

The large proportion of illegal children in the country is caused by the greater liberty of intercourse among youth of both sexes, a greater facility of hiding during the sexual relation, a greater intimacy between the master and the servants . . . lack of other distractions. The largest number of illegitimate children is furnished by daily workers and girls serving in manors or with rich peasants, in houses of officials, etc. . . .

Family [and community] life. . . . People usually confess matters concerning conjugal life or bad example given children, but seldom (almost never) confess negligence in the education of children. For example, a peasant confessed that he beat his wife for not keeping the house and the children clean and not caring for the cattle. . . .

The priest teaches him how to handle his wife to teach her order in a friendly way. Evidently the means are various according to the economical conditions. Sometimes advice to bequeath a morg to the wife if she is clean about the house and cares for the stock or to buy a pretty dress, and to give a good example first of all and not leave everything upon the shoulders of the woman, has an excellent effect. . . . But the greatest influence is exercised by the confessor (if he cares to do it) upon the education of children. One of the priests was a master in this line. He knew how to get out of the peasant the hidden sentiment for the child by [appealing to] his economical point of view as to children and by rousing paternal pride. This priest did not hesitate to make such comparisons as: "Why, are you not proud if your neighbors envy you for having some horse or bull whom you have brought up and whom you keep clean and do not overburden with work? And is your own son, your image and likeness, worse than a bull? Will he not bring more benefit to you later, when he grows up and is strong, wise, and courageous, because you have given him plenty to eat, respected him, and left him time to study? I don't even speak about his soul, image of God Himself. If you feel responsible for your farmstock, if you want order and justice to reign upon the earth, [if you want] the field, the forest, the cattle to serve you, you must care also that your own son or daughter should grow to love this field, this forest, these cattle; you should not make him tired of life and the world by beating him, cursing him, overburdening him with work."

A peasant confesses that he quarrels with his wife. It proves that the man likes to drop into the tavern and that his wife does not like it for she likes money. But he wants to have some distraction "and when one is continually with the women, sometimes an ugly word falls out." And when he returns from the tavern she curses him and he curses her, and she does not want to have anything to do with him and drives him out "to clean his mouth from the smell of liquor and then to come back to her." From anger he goes to a *kuma,* whose husband is night watchman, and sleeps with her sometimes once, sometimes twice a week. Then when he returns home his wife sometimes tries to please him, but then he pushes her away, sometimes striking her, etc.

The ecclesiastical law says that a husband (or wife) who has committed adultery loses the right to demand coitus and only a priest can give him this right back. . . . The priest has to find a *modus vivendi* for them in order to avoid quarrels and to introduce normal relations; he must force the peasant to stop visiting the tavern (pledge not to drink) and try to make each party yield a little. . . .

[The priest acts also as a judge between parties.] The most frequent cases which the confessor must decide are various familial affairs which are either too small or too intimate to carry to the court—"ordinary peasant sins," as once a witty peasant defined them. In these cases the confessor acts not merely as a sacramental judge who decides that something is bad or indifferent and imposes a penance and a satisfaction. Usually he has to hold formal examinations, ask about the behavior of both parties, investigate the circumstances, the situation, use cross-questions in order to study the essence of the matter, and finally pronounce a sentence which determines which person has acted badly and to what extent, and how that person who accuses himself (often he accuses another) has to act in order to redress the wrong done (moral and material) and to settle the familial relations bearably and in a Christian way.

The cause of such quarrels is usually an offence such as the use of something without asking permission, sometimes egotism and an overdeveloped feeling of the right of property and exclusive use of a thing; the most frequent opportunity is gossip and an inborn coarseness in behavior toward the environment. Such quarrels are more frequent and trifling among women. Among men they occur more seldom, mostly about the use of a harness, a rope, a scythe, etc. Sometimes men take sides with women and the "state of war" embraces the whole household. The most characteristic are quarrels about food—flour, grain, bacon, vegetables, which particularly often break out between old and young people—parents and their married children. . . . Although I cannot propose this as a rule, still I have found that in most cases the old people were guilty, started the war. It is not strange. They had worked their whole lives, had raised their children, so they like to eat the children's bread without any work of their own. [The mother helps herself to her daughter's or daughter-in-law's supplies in her absence; the daughter, discovering it, retaliates.] . . . And thus they rob each other. At confession the priest must listen to a whole storeroom litany and reconcile, moderate the angers. Sometimes the daughter does not discover the loss. Then the confessor has to decide whether the mother shall give it back or not. This depends upon the earnings of the son-in-law or the son and on the economic arrangement on which the old people live with the young. . . .

Material profit is always the reason of quarrels, of friendship, guides beliefs, prayers, etc. I had a case where a woman brought during confession money for a mass that her cattle might grow well and her hens lay eggs. The motive was, as proved later, envy of her sister. . . . "Women have told me that she certainly uses charms, . . . but I prefer to address myself to our Lord Jesus in order to have everything better than she." It proved that this woman had also tried charms and wasted time on them instead of working. . . .

A profound mistrust and searching for secret motives of behavior of another person, often ascribing this behavior to "hidden forces," characterize our peasant. Moreover, the lack of wider horizons of interest directs his mind to occultism on the one hand, to an excessive interest in the affairs of neighbors on the other hand. Country gossip, which all the peasant women without exception confess and to which even children show a marked tendency, is precisely a mixture of occultistic beliefs and of criticism of the behavior of neighbors and relatives. Gossip gives birth to slandering, usually called "blackening," that is, spreading of invidious news about neighbors. The background of blackening is either envy . . . or hate, frequently caused by trifling incidents—a petty vanity concerning claims on a church bench; priority in a fraternity or in the community; quarrels of children; refusal to unite two families by wedlock—in a word, hate brought about by considerations of social position.

The use of occult forces is frequently given as a reason of success. There is not any lack either of associations with the devil, charms, etc. A peasant who has given offence to another family must be beforehand prepared for this kind of accusation. In the larger family they are particularly frequent. The motive is very frequently familial diplomacy whose end is material profit—a succession, etc. So again and always—material profit. . . . By what means profit can be reached seems to be an indifferent matter. It is always possible to confess, but it is not always possible to profit—this is the life theory of the peasant, half-cynic (unconsciously), half-Christian . . . full of generous impulses but also of cold calculation. . . .

Christianity requires necessarily interference with the pettiest questions of everyday life in conformity with the principle that it is a doctrine which should not only be recognized but also put into action. . . . The task of the priest in general is to maintain in the mind of the peasant the idea of order in the universe (ascribed to Divine Providence) and to adjust to this idea the performance of all the familial or economical activities. A suitable treatment of the wife, children, parents, and servants, if there are any at home, must be based upon this great harmony of the universe, be connected into one whole, one accord in this harmony, so that everything shall be to the benefit of the family itself (of the head of the family and his wife in first instance) and to the glory of God. The glory of God in the conception of the priest and also of the peasant lies precisely in preserving and developing the order which is one of the manifestations of God's thought in the world. . . . Such teaching . . . sows in a mind that has perhaps never before analyzed its social duties . . . a critical sense and view of functions of life as eating, dressing, spending of money, all kinds of economic transactions, the whole system of private economy, the theory of property, and so on. . . .

Examples: Most frequently the Polish peasant has to be taught about the right of property, about applying honest ideas of property also to the state or to the manor, and about economical justice toward maids or *parobeks* and even toward his own children.

Thus, a peasant confesses that he took some iron [railroad rails and nails] from the road. It is necessary to know that iron of any kind and leather constitute an invincible temptation for our peasant and even a relatively rich peasant will take it, if it is the property of the state. . . . He does not consider it stealing, for this iron is in any case common property [state—all people, in their language]. . . . As difficult a nut to crack for the confessor is teaching the peasants to apply the theory of property also to the orchard, meadow, or field, particularly of the manor and of the priest. . . . Outside of the confessional, the peasant will answer: "God created it for all people," and: "The lord or the priest is rich enough, it won't harm him." . . . In some cases the manor adapts itself to the circumstances. Thus, for example, one manor owner who had very large orchards could not preserve them from thieves. Even the influence of the priest could not stop the robbery. Then the manor owner said to the priest: "Put at least in their heads during confession that they should not break the branches and spoil the trees. . . ."

Sometimes the confession of a peasant who likes to make incursions upon the manorial or communal forest is amusing: "I took some sticks from the forest."—"How many were there?"—"About five."—"Was it brushwood or thicker poles?" No answer. "What did you do with this wood?"—"Well, I repaired the pig-sty and made a few pegs for the fence." The priest begins to suspect that it was a rather serious theft and asks how big and how long were these "sticks" [and finally]: "Were they felled or did you fell them?"—"Well, I did. They were about twice as long as the wagon. But they were communal and therefore also mine." . . . The same applies to the manorial forest, and as to gathering mushrooms and berries (even if it is forbidden), they don't even confess it. The idea that everything is first God's, then people's, and only then the individual's is so strong that the whole pedagogical influence of the priest who proclaims a different principle of property wins very slowly and very few adherents. "The priest talks so because it is suitable for him." These few words illustrate well the relation between the priest and the peasants in this field. . . .

Reformatory character of the confessor's influence. . . . Confession is in many cases a powerful reformatory factor in social evils such as alcoholism, theft, immoral behavior, etc. [There is marked improvement throughout Poland, particularly as regards alcoholism.] . . . Certainly other social factors play also a certain part such as more enlightenment, social organization, and social action against liquor-shops. But these factors have only a preventive value. Where the problem is how to eradicate an inveterate evil, confession—the force of religious beliefs—must be added to a common social activity if positive results are to be obtained.

The influence of confession is strengthened by suitable sermons and teachings. They prepare also the way for breaking and converting the obstinate. But confession is always the moment of crisis and even if in individual cases it does not bring a definite victory, in any case it undermines the force of the bad habit. This extraordinary influence of confession lies (1) in its ordinary psychological action, and (2) in its supernatural, magical "charm," connected with the fear of the judgment of God, the feeling of the unworthiness of the vice, and the hope of pardon through confession. The personal force of the confessor's action is also based upon two types of factors—his natural cleverness and ability to influence others, and upon the magical powers which the faith of the penitent ascribes to him. The method of action depends on the individual, on his disposition, and on the force of the habit . . . it must be different in almost every particular case. . . . The situation presents itself frequently as a war in which the drunkard fights for his dose, the priest for the physical and spiritual good of this drunkard. But the drunkard fights alone or in alliance with only a few friends, while on the side of the priest stands the whole coalition of the members of the family, the magical forces, the prayers and sacrifices of the wife and children (often heroic), the punishing and excluding hand of the church, and the opinion of the majority of the community. . . .

Written for the authors by a Galician priest
who wishes his name withheld.

LETTERS TO THE COMMUNITY NEWSPAPER

I am sending a brief remembrance of my youth. There is no interesting adventure in question, but I think it will interest the readers as a proof that if one urgently and perseveringly desires something he attains it in the end, at least in part. I am the son of a peasant farmer. Until 10 years of age I did not know the alphabet, or exactly speaking, I knew only the letter B. Father did not send me to school. He always used to repeat: "We have grown old and we cannot read nor write, yet we live. So you, my children, will also live without knowledge." Nothing could have suited me better. In the winter I went sledging with the boys and in summer I pastured geese.

Once my mother took me to church. I looked to the right; a boy smaller than myself was praying from a book. I looked to the left; another one just like the first held a book, and I stood between them like a ninny. I went home and told my father that I would learn from a book. My father scolded me: "And who will peel potatoes in the winter and pasture the geese in summer?" I cried then because I felt ashamed that I should grow up and not know how to read.

Once while peeling potatoes, I escaped from my father and went to an old man who knew not only how to read, but how to write well. I asked him to show me [letters] in the primer, and he did not refuse. I went home thinking: "It's too bad! Father will probably give me a licking." And it came true. Father showered a few strokes on me and said: "Snotty fellow, don't you know that, as the old people say, whoever learns written stuff casts himself into hell?" But I stole out to learn more and more frequently. The following winter father did not forbid it, and slowly I learned how to read and write.

When I was twelve years old, I had already read various books, but only fables, for at that time one could most frequently find in the village books like *Ali Baba, Sobotnia Góra*, etc. Once I found an old almanac on the road. I looked at it and on the last page read that there was in Warsaw a *Gazeta Świąteczna* which people order and receive by mail every Sunday. After that I said to one of the neigh-

---

4:223–25, 228–31, 234–37, 253–54, 261–65.

bors—not a young man: "Do you know, in Warsaw there is a *Gazeta* which every one, even if not educated, can read!" And that man said to me: "Look at him, the snotty fellow! He wants a newspaper!" He said to my father: "Do you know, *kum,* your son will become a real lord, for he says that he will order a newspaper."—"Ho, ho!" said my father, "but where will he get the money?"

After some time father turned me from pasturing geese to tending cattle. Once another herdsman told me that there was in Suchedniów, not far from our village, a railroad watchman whose name was Korzec, and that he had the *Gazeta.* I immediately gave my cattle to someone else to tend and rushed to Korzec. When I came in he asked me: "What do you want, boy?"—"I came to see what the *Gazeta* to which you seem to subscribe looks like." He showed me the *Gazeta Świąteczna.* I began to read and liked it very much. All right, but where shall I get the money for it?

I began to make brooms and sell them at 3 grosz apiece; I plaited whips, and in this way between spring and St. John's Day I saved 2 złoty. But that was not enough. Where could I get some more? It was hard to get away from the cattle to earn something. Once I was pasturing the cattle near a colony in the forest. Some strangers approached and one said to me: "Boy, do you know how to read? I would give you a book with interesting stories." I answered that I could and thanked him for the book, but at the same time I asked bashfully for a little money. "You rogue," said the stranger, "what do you need money for?" I said for the *Gazeta.* But he replied: "Perhaps for cigarettes?"—"No," said I crying, "I have already 2 złoty and I need 15 grosz more to have 2½ złoty, and the carpenter says that he will contribute as much more and that would be just enough for a quarter. . . . I took an oath at my first confession that I would not drink whiskey nor smoke cigarettes until twenty-one years old." Then that gentleman took out and gave me not 15 grosz, but as much as 3 złoty and also the book [saying], "Here you will have enough to subscribe alone to the *Gazeta* for a whole quarter." How great was my joy would be hard to describe. I immediately asked a boy to write to the editor for the *Gazeta,* and the following Sunday I already had it in the house. As soon as they saw it in the village they began to say various things about it that only lords ought to read the *Gazeta,* that reading takes time. But I did not listen to them and only read with great delight.

I have now subscribed to the *Gazeta* for 8 years. I no longer lack money for it, as for the last 6 years I have been a forester and live on a farm of 15 morgs. I have grown so accustomed to the *Gazeta* that when Sunday comes I have in one hand the spoon and in the other the *Gazeta*. People say that reading the *Gazeta* requires a lot of time. But on a holiday there is not time enough for both praying and reading? . . . And I say that a peasant in the country needs the *Gazeta* more than one who has already been enlightened in school. We certainly can draw knowledge from the *Gazeta*. It is true that there are some newspapers which are not written for everybody, but as if in a foreign language [using learned words]. However, I am speaking about one which everyone, even an uneducated, simple man, can understand. . . . I often say: "If it should be necessary to eat only once a day, I will do it, but I will not cease subscribing to the *Gazeta* until the end of my life."

In conclusion, I send a hearty "God reward" to Priest Woźniako-weski for having forbidden me to smoke cigarettes. I never learned how to let money go up in smoke. Therefore I am able to subscribe to the *Gazeta*. I also send "God reward" to Marcin Korzec for having shown me the way to the *Gazeta*.

Gazeta Świąteczna, 1898, 31.

My wife did not remain behind Antoni's and Jan's wives. . . . I have not been a reader of *Gazeta* for a very long time; I got it for the first time only in 1895. Then it was easier for me, because then my wife did not understand what this paper meant. But when she perceived a piece of paper, out of which, according to her understanding, there was no profit, she started to make a row. So on every occasion I had always something to swallow. I had taunts and curses: "May you break your neck! May you get blind, you damned newspaperman! . . . Fixes his eyes [into the paper] and looks like a crow at an old bone. . . ."

There were such rumblings and murmurs all the time. But I endured it all. I did not growl with anger, I only laughed at her silly talk. And when she talked too much, I used to withdraw from her sight and I pitied her lack of sense. But what do you require from an ox if not meat? I was not even surprised, because in their family nobody knew how to read and therefore the daughter was brought up like a calf behind a stove.

One year passed; the time came to order the *Gazeta,* and then it would have been impossible to say even "brum-brum" to the wife about that! But the neighbor who was taking my paper to read during the first year said to me: "See, I will pay for this year and we will read it together." Well, and so it happened.

When I brought the *Gazeta* and began to read, my wife always talked with somebody as loud as she could or asked me about something in order to disturb me as much as possible. My friends used to come to me to learn what news the *Gazeta* brought. When they asked me I used to reply: "I do not know. I read hastily so that it did not leave very much in my memory and I had to give the *Gazeta* away at once. But ask my wife. She can tell you more because she walks quietly, notices everything attentively, and can remember well."

In the beginning I got for this many a time a good reprimand from my wife, but if she did not dare to scold me in the presence of the guest she became ashamed and blushed from anger and left the house. Gradually she grew silent during the time of my reading in order to remember something and to tell when asked. It became a little easier for me because my wife stopped scolding me. I began to read to her some funny stories or some adventures described in *Gazeta* and many times she even laughed heartily. Then again I read to her the *Lives of the Saints,* and at these times she was often moved to tears and wept not a little. And I was very glad that it grew clearer in her head and that she began to respect books.

In the fall of 1897 I moved from the country into the town. I bought a house with a piece of garden, but everything had been devastated by my predecessor. I had to prepare everything according to my way and therefore I was glancing continually into my file and I was altering everything possible. But it was necessary to get the paper again so as to complete my education in farming. I asked the wife whether she would allow me [to get the paper]. And the wife answered: "Well, if you want to. Instead of running to town and fooling there, you will stay at home and read. Besides they write there how to cultivate the soil for vegetables so that we can arrange everything ourselves in the garden and everywhere." And she allowed me to order the paper for 1898, but on condition that I should not smoke cigarettes. I consented. . . .

When I received the *Gazeta* I read all the news and told my wife

how, what, and when to do [things] and we began to work. We planted gooseberries, raspberries, shrubs for grafting; in the garden we
made paths, we manured and dug around the soil, and we planted
vegetables. I also got from the priest some flower seeds. . . . My wife
laughs when she hears that people take us for gardeners and rejoic-
es because they praise our work. And all this she owes to the *Gazeta
Świąteczna*. She began to learn herself and now she reads not very
badly. Even our 5-year-old daughter is beginning to decipher the
primer because her mother forces her to, not wanting her to be ig-
norant as she was herself until now. And she does not forbid me to
use the money not only for the *Gazeta* but even for books, if they are
but useful. God forbid that I read it silently! Whenever I read it must
be quiet at home, and she pays eager attention to everything. . . .

So, let the readers behave mildly with their wives, just as I; let
them read the *Gazeta* carefully and intelligently, and let them show
by example what the benefit of their reading is. Let the woman see
how much good may be done by conforming to what good people
describe and advise. . . . But if you read the paper under your nose
for yourself, or if after reading you throw it into the corner; if you
read it only for play, or if you subscribe to the *Gazeta* only to show
off before the neighbors, and if after reading nothing is left in your
head . . . well, what wonder that the woman scolds?

Letter to Gazeta Świąteczna, published,
but reference not preserved.

I am a country housewife. . . . I have three little children that
need continual care. Before the infant school was opened I had a
lot of trouble with these children and could not manage them. They
were always running around the roads with other children and paid
almost no attention to my calls and threats; they were pointblank
obstinate and disobedient. At one time, even in spite of my order
to the contrary, they went out on the street and after a while there
came to my ears a shriek from the children. The cause of it was that
a farmer had run down one of my children. Thanks to God Al-
mighty, the child suffered no injuries.

Always anxious about my children, I had not a moment of ease.
At last God took pity upon us unfortunate mothers and caused good
people, willing to come with aid to their fellow men, to take up the
idea of establishing an infant school in Pilica. This was done. I am

sending two of my children to this nursery. There they remain almost the whole day. There they study to do fancy work and learn to speak little verses. What is most important, they study religion, how to respect their parents and elders and how to be polite. They have attended the school for a year and a half already and everyone associating with them admires them and says: "What pleasant and polite children! They are like angels." And there is reason to praise them. When they meet some one they know, they will bow and the girls bend their right leg a little; the boys remove their caps.

During long winter evenings the children meet at my house (those that attend the school) and so do the neighbors. The children entertain us for the whole evening. One of them reads, the next one recites, and another displays her fancy work, still another one sings, and so on. At nine o'clock they all depart, very pleased and happy. This year on my name-day my children presented their congratulations to me. How pleasant it was to hear the recitation of my daughter! How I enjoyed the children's gift! . . .

The school teachers chose from among the children attending the school a few that have pleasant voices, among whom are also my children, and taught them different religious songs. And now they sing in the choir at the parochial church in Pilica. Formerly a few male voices roared coarsely and unintelligibly, and now it is pleasant in our church when the children sing. Just after the [feast of] the Three Kings *Jasełka* was played for us, and this also by our children. The young actors and actresses played their parts very successfully. The public rewarded them with frequent applause and praise.

We mothers are very much surprised how the teachers of the school can make such polite and obedient children from such obstinate and impolite ones. We know that it must cost them much, very much labor and exertion; therefore, with every prayer we beg God to grant them all graces.

Letter to *Ziemianka*, unpublished.

There were never yet so many readers in Chocianowice as on Sunday, September 5th. Like lightning the news spread in the village that our village was described in *Gazeta Świąteczna* under the title, "Growth of Drinking." Almost everybody, old and young, knew on this Sunday and passed the word that somebody had writen to *Gazeta* about

Chocianowice. Honest people praised the man who wrote and said he did very well; others cursed and promised to take revenge on the man who wrote. But those who sell the poison were moved most. One shopkeeper took it to heart so much that he resolved to sell this accursed whiskey no more, and did not sell it; when anyone came to buy this poison the man said: "If I am to be described in the *Gazeta*, I will sell no more." So everybody left with an empty bottle and with a full pocket, and with a curse, not against the man who did not give him vodka, but against the one who wrote to the *Gazeta*. That seller did well, but it was done only in order that people who wanted vodka might come to him once more and beg him [to sell].

Then people resolved to guess who was the man who wrote that letter to *Gazeta*, and they decided not to forgive him when they guessed it. Well, after long trouble they guessed the riddle: "It must be that one [the writer] because he has read the *Gazeta* for a long time, he does not drink vodka, and there is nobody else in the village [like him]." Only they have not carried out their threat, perhaps because that [shopkeeper] sold his resolution to them, like Judas. He justifies himself that he is earning his living, and his allies say yes.

And now I confess that you guessed right who wrote [the letter]. You say that I don't smoke cigarettes and don't drink vodka, and it is true, but I owe it to *Gazeta Świąteczna*, because it led me to enlightenment. Now only I know how to live, how to love my Polish brethren, and how to root out drinking. Further, you say that I slander you. But I had never the idea of slandering you; you slander yourselves. It was clearly written in the *Gazeta* that more than a half [of the villagers] are good and honest. Is it my fault if you don't want to belong to these good and honest farmers? I step out openly against my enemy and my enemy is drink. . . . Through drinking you become enemies of our fatherland. So, if you have at least a spark of love for your mother, the Polish land, you will stand together with these honest men and cry: "Away with drinking and revelry in our village!"

Letter to *Gazeta Świąteczna*, unpublished.

[The following letter shows how indispensable for individual self-control the backing of the community is, but also how the wider community can be substituted for the primary group.]

In 1887 I read in the *Gazeta* a beautiful and useful article under the title: "To smoke or not to smoke." I read attentively and agreed that it was true. And as I was a habitual smoker—for I smoked ⅜ of a pound of *machorka* a week—this truth made me reflect seriously. I wondered what to do. "Don't smoke," cried my reason. But how to eradicate the accursed habit?

I tried to persuade my neighbors to renounce smoking; I read to them what good and wise people wrote about it. My neighbors answered that they could not stop smoking, for they were "too much used to it, and the loss does not matter, because those who do not smoke are no wealthier." Some also told such a tale: A man who smoked ceased to smoke and put aside the pennies which he had been spending on smoking, until he had economized 9 roubles. With this money he bought a pig and used all his grain in feeding him. The pig died and the man suffered hunger.

But I succeeded in persuading the most enlightened one among my neighbors, F. Pr. We read again that article in the *Gazeta* and at the command: "One, two, three," we threw our pipes on the ground. We threw into the fire our stores of tobacco and promised to try not to smoke for two months, or at least to buy nothing to smoke. We kept our resolution, but after two months we began to buy and to smoke. But since that time I have been an enemy of smoking. I smoked, but only because I could not withstand temptation. I went into company; one or another treated me with cigarettes and it was difficult to renounce such a treat. But several times I did not smoke for three or four months at once, from spring until autumn. . . . But none of my neighbors would follow my example, and as in winter they come to my house twice a week to have a talk, I, seeing them smoking, took my pipe, too.

Last spring, having read in the *Gazeta* opinions of doctors about the harmfulness of smoking, I took them to heart, explained to my neighbors, and on April 5 definitely ceased smoking. Under the eyes of my neighbors, I carried my pipe to the fire and said: "You were burning, destroying my health. Now I am overcoming you, fiend. Get burned, disappear, be lost!" . . . Two neighbors promise to stop smoking, but somehow they still hesitate. . . .

We readers of the *Gazeta*, though our number is still small compared with those who do not read, although scattered throughout the whole world and not acquainted personally with one another, can boldly consider ourselves real brothers, for we have been educated spiritually and we are taken care of by the one *Gazeta Świąteczna*. Let us then listen to her[*Gazeta* is feminine gender in Polish] advice, explanations, and exhortations with childlike faith and confidence. Let us take into consideration that the nineteenth year is already approaching its end since the *Gazeta* began to teach us, showing us good and evil; and thus we are approaching our majority and can think for ourselves about our lot and one brother ask another: "To smoke or not to smoke?" . . .

I would not write at all about my not smoking, for I do not demand any praise; but I publish this as an example and in order to incite my fellow readers to do likewise. . . . It would be well if neighbors or even more distant readers gave one another a word, a promise not to smoke. Such an association gives encouragement; in company everybody is more cheerful.

Gazeta Świąteczna, 1899, 38.

Dear Sisters: We read often in popular papers how our brothers are called to social work and to learning. These appeals are, indeed, very just. But nevertheless in reading them we feel some pain, even some jealousy. Why are only brothers called to work, to learning? And we women, have we the right, ought we to remain in darkness and in social inactivity? Never! It is high time for us women to awake spiritually. Therefore, let us, sisters, call one another to learning and to work for the rebirth of the land. . . . It is a shame for us women that we keep away from such work and even, alas! that we divert our husbands from it.

Who is most to blame that in villages and towns we have almost no kindergartens and no schools for children? Who is principally guilty that our consumers' associations and Polish shops have little success? Who is at fault that our husbands read little and our children avoid the school? I will say positively: *Only we, the women.* Our women don't care for kindergartens and schools, they pass indifferently by the the consumers' shops. We are angry with our husbands and sons when they spend money for papers and books, and often we don't send our children to school and we keep them at home for any trifling reason, for the sake of some work which somebody else could do. If our son or our daughter wants to go to a farm school, we withhold them because there is work at home and we pretend that we have no money. . . .

Our people is unhappy, dark, powerless, in misery and humiliation. But to a large extent we could avoid our misfortunes, many could easily remove totally their painful penury. For the larger part of our soil is fertile, much wealth is in the earth, much work in the land, but people of strange birth and faith draw all the benefits for themselves, and we, the children of Lech, the children of this soil, which our fathers and grandfathers bathed with their blood, we are in poverty, in neglect, and we look for bread, for wages far away from our fatherland, from our beloved Poland. We, the Polish women, could remedy it if we would and if we knew how to do it. We ought not to boast, but in conformity with the truth we must acknowledge that our husbands respect us and often do as we advise, or simply yield to our claims for the sake of peace—although not all of them.

So we have a great influence in private and in social matters, and therefore it is to a large extent our fault if things go badly with us. But unhappily many women don't acknowledge this fault. Often we care more for nice dresses and hats than for social and national questions, and this is very bad. In this manner we do a serious wrong to society without knowing it. But this unconsciousness does not diminish our fault at all; on the contrary, it makes it greater still because it is the consequence of negligence, of a blameworthy sluggishness and, I dare say, of an aversion to enlightenment and to progress in general. . . .

Zorza, 1914, 10.

PART
2
THE PEASANT LETTERS

The peasant letters are the heart of *The Polish Peasant*. The original book contained letters from fifty families organized to show both the disintegrating effect of capitalist development on the family and the rebuilding of the family in the process of immigration. The mere existence of the letters shows that the immigrants kept their families together, even when they became geographically as well as culturally separated. In addition, these letters are human documents of incomparable significance.

Thomas and Znaniecki's viewpoint was that traditional Polish community life was held together by familial ties termed "mutual help," meaning obligations that individuals felt toward one another by virtue of family position. In the Polish village, they argue, economic considerations were not as important as social ones. The spread of the market and the evolution of what they call a "climbing mentality" changed the family through the "growing assertion of the personality." While this created familial conflicts, for example, children became harder to control, it also created new possibilities for personal development.

The first series of letters, by the Wróblewski family, illustrates the tensions created by the breakup of the traditional family. The father, Walery, thinks only of his wish to remarry and will not consider the interests of the family as a whole. All the family members, including those working in America, become involved in the problem.

The Markiewicz series concerns "climbers." The writers' interest centers on the two sons, Wacław and Maks, who have migrated to the United States. Wacław has become a socialist and an atheist, whereas Maks is economically ambitious. According to Thomas and Znaniecki, the spread of a cash economy gave rise to a "new idea which we may term the standard of living: its essence lies in the power which the individual has over his economic environment by virtue of his income." The decisive moment in Maks Markiewicz's evolution from peasant to worker, according to Thomas and Znaniecki, came when he purchased a watch.

The Raczkowski series centers on two children's adaptation to American conditions. Adam uses his new position to sustain the older ideals of familial solidarity and to lord it over his sisters. Helena, who has married, finds it difficult to control her children without the support provided in Poland by strong family and community ties.

Finally, in the Borkowski series, Władysław has emigrated and is going to bring his wife to the United States. We only have her letters, but it is apparent that she waited the rest of her life for his summons. Probably he remarried, though he retains obligations to her. As Thomas and Znaniecki point out, she is weak because she is isolated: they were city dwellers in Poland. Had they come from a rural community, her husband would have been forced by the community to meet his obligations and she, in turn, would have been supported emotionally until he did.

The section begins with a statement by Thomas and Znaniecki concerning these peasant letters, and in introductory sections to each letter group, and in footnotes, they try to indicate the letters' significance.

The Polish peasant writes many and long letters. This is particularly striking, since the business of writing or even of reading letters is at best very difficult for him [*sic*]. It requires a rather painful effort of reflection and sacrifice of time. Letter writing is for him a social duty of a ceremonial character, and the traditional, fixed form of peasant letters is a sign of their social function.

All the peasant letters can be considered as variations of one fundamental type, whose form results from its function and remains always essentially the same, even if it eventually degenerates. We call this type the "bowing letter."

The bowing letter is normally written by or to a member of the family who is absent for a certain time. Its function is to manifest the persistence of familial solidarity in spite of the separation. Such an expression became necessary only when members of the family began to leave their native locality; as long as the family stayed in the same community, the solidarity was implicitly and permanently assumed. The whole group manifested its unity at periodical and extraordinary meetings, but no single member in particular was obliged to manifest his own familial feelings more than other members, unless on some extraordinary occasions, e.g., at the time of his or her marriage. But the individual who leaves his family finds himself in a distinctive situation as compared with that of other members, and the bowing letter is the product of this situation. There is nothing corresponding to it in personal, immediate familial relations.

In accordance with its function the bowing letter has an exactly determined composition. It begins with the religious greeting: "Praised be Jesus Christus," to which the reader is supposed to answer, "In centuries of centuries. Amen." The greeting has both a magical and a moral significance. Magically it averts evil; morally it shows that the writer and the reader are members of the same religious community, and from the standpoint of the moral-religious

---

1:303–4.

system every community is religious. A common subordination to God may also be otherwise expressed throughout the entire letter, but the greeting is the most indispensable expression. There follows the information that the writer, with God's help, is in good health and is succeeding, and he wishes the same for the reader and the rest of the family. We know that health (struggle against death) and living constitute the reason of natural and human solidarity (only spiritual solidarity aims at power). Finally come greetings, "bows," for all the members of the family, or from all the members of the family if the letter is written to the absent member. The enumeration should be complete, embracing at least all the members who still live in the same locality, if the family is already scattered, as often happens today.

These elements remain in every letter, even when the function of the letter becomes more complicated; every letter, in other words, whatever else it may be, is a bowing letter, a manifestation of solidarity. Various elements may be schematized; the words "bows for the whole family," for example, may be substituted for the long enumeration, but the principle remains unchanged in all the familial letters.

WRÓBLEWSKI SERIES

The Wróblewskis live in the northeastern part of ethnographical Poland, in a relatively poor province. The family (whose real name we do not use) belongs to the peasant nobility and is relatively well instructed. It has lived in the same village since at least the fifteenth century. Twelve neighboring villages are chiefly occupied by descendants of the same ancestors, though their names have been partly diversified. The community of origin has probably been in a large measure forgotten. The main figure of the series is Walery Wróblewski, the author of most of the letters. [Their main subject concerns] Walery's relation to his father and brothers on the ground of the problem of inheritance. In this relation Walery, the oldest

---

1:316.

brother, as against the father and partly against Feliks [his brother], represents the old principles of familial solidarity—according to which the family should act harmoniously as a whole, and the father should pursue the interests of this whole, not his own egotistic ends—and of justice—according to which the economic problems should be settled upon a moral as against a merely legal basis. This relation is expanded and complicated by the new marriage of the father. The stepmother is not an isolated individual, but the member of another family, and the antagonism of interests prevents her absolute assimilation into her husband's family. On the contrary, as no harmonious coexistence of the two families is possible, it is the husband, Walery's father, who loses all connection with his own family and becomes assimilated to his wife's family. . . . The father's fundamental feature, by which his whole behavior is explained, is the powerful desire to live a personal life up to the end, in spite of the tradition which requires the father to be the bearer of the familial idea and to resign his claims on the control of economic and general familial matters when he is partly invalided by age and unable to manage those matters for the greatest benefit of the family.[1] In his struggle against this tradition, the old Wróblewski finally has no course other than to resign completely his place in his own family. In fact he becomes a stranger and can thus live an unimpeded personal life.

1. In this regard there is a striking likeness between him and Franciszka Kozłowska (cf. that series, 2:1–16, 24), with this difference: Kozłowska, as a woman, was never called upon to be the representative of the familial idea.

THE FAMILY WRÓBLEWSKI

Wróblewski, a farmer
Klimusia, his third wife
Walery, his son
Józef, his son
Antoni (Antoś), his son (lives in America)
Konstanty (Kostuś), his son (lives in America)
Feliks, his son (lives in Russia)

1:325–32, 335–37, 339, 341–48, 351–53, 365, 374–75.

From Walery Wróblewski in Poland, to His Brothers in America,
With a Last Letter from Józef

ŁAPY, January 2, 1906

DEAR BROTHERS: [Usual greetings and generalities about health.] Your letter of October 29 I received on December 30. It traveled for about 2 months, and perhaps it lay in the post offices, because there has been a strike. All the trains stopped for more than a week, and afterward in the post and telegraph service there was a strike for 3 weeks. "Strike" means in our language *bezrobocie* and in Russian *zabastowka* ["stopping of work"]. It happens now very often among us, particularly in factories. Workmen put forward their demands. They want higher pay and a shorter working day; they refuse to work more than 8 hours a day. Now everything has become terribly dear, particularly with shoemakers and tailors. . . . Even now there is no order in the country, the whole time tumults about liberty are going on, because on October 30 the Highest Manifesto was proclaimed concerning personal inviolability, liberty of the press, etc. In a word, by favor of the monarch we have more liberty, because we are citizens of the country, not as formerly, when we were only subjects; now we are all equal in the country. Papers are published without censure, so they now write more truth, only all this is not yet fixed. The liberty of speech has also been given by the Highest Manifesto, and for this reason different songs are sung, as "Boże coś Polskę. . . ." In short, thanks to God, conditions would not be bad, but still much trouble can happen, because there is no peace in the land, and even terrible things happen, as in Moscow and many other towns.[1] . . .

1. The revolution of 1905–6 contributed greatly to the development of social consciousness and interest in political problems among the peasants. Up to this time those interests in Russian Poland were developed artificially, by patriotic agitation from the intelligent classes. Indeed, the relative simplicity and isolation of peasant life, together with the bureaucratic organization of the Russian state, made it hardly possible for the peasant to understand that there was any relation between the real interests of his life and the more general political problems. The communal self-government allowed, within certain limits, the settlement of most of the problems of everyday life, but outside of the commune the peasant had no influence upon social and political life, and thus all the phenomena whose source lay in the state and in the economic organization—law, military service, taxes, school organization, official language, means of communication, and prices of natural and manufactured

products—appeared to him as regulated once and forever by a superior and unde-termined force. His attitude toward them was more or less like his attitude toward the weather—fundamentally passive resignation, with sometimes an attempt to in-fluence with prayer or gift the powers in their treatment of the individual's own sphere of interests. The revolution of 1905–6 showed the peasant that this assumed order is modifiable and may be influenced directly and in its organization by hu-man will; it showed at the same time unknown and unsuspected relations between many apparently abstract problems and the facts of everyday life.

April 2, 1906

DEAR BROTHERS: . . . . We will divide with you in thought at least the consecrated food [*święcone*]. It is a pity that you will probably have no *święcone*, because you are surely far away from the church. Well, it cannot be helped; you will probably only remember our country and nothing more.[1] But perhaps our Lord God will allow you to return happily; then we shall rejoice. . . .

As to the money, when I receive it I will do as you wrote; I will give 10 roubles to father and will keep by me the remaining 240, or I will put it somewhere until you come back. Meanwhile my chil-dren thank their uncle for the remembrance and the promise. Spring approaches, but although it is already April, weather is bad, it snows every day. Some people have seen storks already; they must be wretched, walking upon white [snow].[2] . . .

I wrote you what I could about our country, although in short, for if I wanted to write in detail, I should need many sheets of pa-per. Now, please, write us about the mines. How are the passages to them made under the earth? Are there any props? What happens when coal is dug out—whether they [the passages] fall in or stand? In short, whatever may be new for us.[3] . . .

W. WRÓBLEWSKI

1. The Easter wishes, dividing the *święcone* with the thought of absent relatives, are evidently means of preserving the family connection in spite of separation, and in the particular form which this connection assumes in group festivals.

2. An example of the sympathy of the peasant with animals. The peasant sto-ries show that this sympathy developed to a very high degree.

3. Here, as in many other similar questions, it seems as if the interest of the writer were purely objective, i.e., not determined by the fact that the conditions about which he asks are those in which his relatives live. But the *effect* is evidently the constitution of a new common field of intellectual life and thus the mainte-nance of the group connection, whether this was the conscious aim or not.

June 30, 1906

DEAR BROTHERS: . . . . Now I inform you how farming is going on at home. Well, it turns out that Feliks cannot get along with the old people. Although he *does* work, he plows and carts manure, in short, he does everything necessary in farming, yet under the management of the old man it is impossible to work. He must dress himself and his children, and live, but the old man does not give any money; he keeps everything himself. He does not even give possible food. He wants to drive them away in this way the soonest possible, and that will probably happen very soon, and the old man will again sell [parts of his land] and gratify himself and the old woman. It will be enough for them both [the land will last as long as they last]. And now the quarreling is incessant. "Why did they come?" But he wanted them to come, because he said, "I sell the ground because there is nobody to work." And now, "Do as you please and get your living where you please!" So Feliks will be obliged to seek a job, and father will farm on in the old way, until there will not be a single lot of land left. If he lives long, then finally a bag and a stick only will remain from this farming, and that will be our only inheritance, because there is no possibility of getting along with father. . . .

W. WRÓBLEWSKI

July 5, 1906

DEAR BROTHER: . . . . I mentioned about brother Feliks, how they are farming at home. Now I will write you still more. As I wrote already, father gave him the farm to manage, but this lasted perhaps for two days; then father took it again into his hands. And then began the misery and quarreling. Feliks complains that he was wronged, that he lost his employment, and now father gives him nothing. He was angry with me, because I wrote him that father intended to give him [the management of the farm] and now he does not give it, or rather he gave it, but took it away. I began also to claim for their sake, that father was acting badly—first so, then otherwise. Then father said, "If it is my fault, I will will them Kopciowizna [some part of the farm]. Let them work and help me to the end, then they will have this as a reward." I did not oppose this strongly, only I said that I could not decide alone, but that I must write to you and ask what you say, and meanwhile wait. So I wrote, but I have no answer yet, and they did not wait. At home they quarrel continually; Feliks complains about his misery, that he has enough work but not enough to eat—that father gives them nothing to eat. Feliksowa [wife of Feliks] comes to me several times a day, and every time with a new complaint. Things went so far that Feliks and father took knives and axes. And she runs frequently to me, saying once that father wants to beat them, then again that he wants to drive them away from his home with hunger. Evidently, I did not praise father for all this. But whatever I said against father, Feliksowa reported it so to father that I [seem to] incite her against him, and she complained to father against me. At last all their knavery and meanness appeared clearly. . . . When brother Józef came, he told me that when they quarreled with father, father gave the whole secret up and confessed it himself. He said, "I wronged the other [children] and willed you Kopciowizna, and this is your gratitude?"[1] Up to this time all was done secretly; we did not know anything about it, neither I nor Józef. Then I understood the whole thing in a different way, and I told Feliks everything about their meanness. I brought their anger upon me; they were provoked with me for telling them, "You have robbed us all, because you have done it secretly."[2] He said that father had forbidden them to tell. They circumvented father in some way during the fair in Sokoły, and father willed [the land] to them in such a way, that now he will own this up to his death, and after his death it will be theirs, as a gift from father, the remainder of the farm to be divided equally. After that they quit boarding with father and yesterday they moved over to Józef Pilat, and live there. What happens later I will inform you in due time. I hear that they plan a law suit against father and me for indemnity for their pretended wrongs.

. . . . Please write us your opinion about this affair. Perhaps this letter will find itself among the documents of Feliks? [Perhaps you will concert with Feliks against me and send him this letter.] But I don't believe it.

I remain respectfully yours, but writing always the truth

W. WRÓBLEWSKI

1. This act of the old man was evidently done with the intention of assuring himself of the alliance of at least one son against the others and of getting rid of his control without making him an enemy. It proves that the old man did not feel

his position very strong morally, although he had legally full right to do as he pleased with his farm.

2. The secrecy is particularly bad, because to the economic wrong is added a social wrong—destruction of the familial solidarity.

July 27, 1906

DEAR BROTHER: . . . . Now I inform you about home and the conflict with Feliks. If you received my letter, you know already how it was about the willing of Kopciowizna—how they did it secretly with father, then how they quarreled with father, how he moved to the house of Józef Pilat. Now she remains here with her children, and he went to the old place in search of employment. He does not write me anything, because we are angry with each other. I told him that such things ought not to be done by cunning, but that he could have done all this so that everybody might know. He excuses himself, on the ground that father forbade him to mention anything to us about his having willed [the land] to them. But even now I don't know whether there is in this will any mention about the mill; probably not, and then I must move it away from that lot. Father is farming as he did formerly; he hires harvesters and drives the crops from the field, but I don't know how long this will last. When the old man goes to bed I don't know how he will do the farming. Feliks has received his part already, and if the old man does not change it, he will still receive an equal part with us. What ought we to do? I ask you beforehand, how are we to act? In my opinion he ought to have only this lot and nothing more, and father ought to divide the remainder among us. Judge yourself. . . .

W. W.

August 27, 1906

DEAR BROTHER: . . . . Józef told me that he also received a letter from you. Whether he answered I don't know, but he says that he is unwilling to go to America, because he has it here well enough. Now you ask me for advice, whether you ought to remain in the mines, or to return home, or to search for other work in America. Well I leave the decision with you, but in my opinion it would be dangerous to throw your work away just now, but rather [I advise you] to search first for other work in America and then to come back about spring, or to remain where you are meanwhile and then to come back. But don't take my advice. Whatever you do will be well, because I fear it may be as with Feluś, though I don't believe that you could be so mean as he.[1] He curses me now ceaselessly for his own meanness. I wrote to him also: "If you are to come, first think it over thoroughly lest you regret it later." (And he [answered]: "I must move to my country for my children's sake.") And what has resulted? He robbed us all, and he continually slanders me and father. The old man is somewhat guilty in not having given him what he promised; but he rewarded him, even more than his right, in the will. And what does he want from me? I have heard that he abuses me also in the letters which he writes to her [his wife], saying that he suffers misery by my fault. And why does he abuse me? Because I said the truth openly, that it is unfair to act in such a thievish manner; everybody ought to know what you intend to do.

1. The responsibility of an adviser for the consequences of his advice is particularly great when the personal influence of the adviser is great because the peasant gives to the advice a consideration proportionate to the prestige of the adviser rather than the intrinsic value of the advice. In the present case the advice of Walery is the more weighty because he is the oldest brother.

October 29, 1906

DEAR BROTHER: . . . . I received your second letter also, from which I learned about your misfortune, the bruising of your arms.

Now I inform you first, that I intend to remain at home this year, unless any unforeseen circumstances happen. I do nothing but plan about my house. . . . Feliksowa has left again and went there to him [Feliks], having sold her things to Józef Pilat. She sold the cow also which father gave them, because she lived in Pilat's house. She went like a swine, because she called neither on me nor on father before leaving for the forests. That is just where she ought to live, with bears, not with men. She was something of an ape before, and there she became altogether an ape. No honest person would have done as they did. Whose fault is it? And how much they have cursed me, and father! May God not punish them for it. They think only about a fortune and money and don't want anything else; they don't regard church-going and fasting, if only they can live comfortably in this world.

Now in our country disorders still go on, sometimes robberies, sometimes killing with bombs or revolvers.

[W. Wróblewski]

February 24, 1907

Dear Brother: . . . . I received . . . your . . . letter of February 4, in which you tell about your misfortune and write that I caused you a great displeasure by my letter—that I gave you the last blow. Believe me, if I had known that it would reach you when you were in such a condition, I would have chosen not to mention anything, but who could have expected anything like this? . . . If I made some reproaches, your own letter induced me to do it. You wrote that you keep company in which you cannot get along for a single day without beer or whisky. Then I wanted to draw you back from it, and therefore I made some remarks—that this money would be useful here, and for whom [it would be useful].[1] I had also had no idea, that you had any difficulties in sending money. I know only this, that if somebody has money and wants to send it, and has anybody to whom he may send it, he does send it, and does not write that it is difficult, unless he has none. But what happened between us is quite ridiculous. Well, never mind, let it be as you do it. Today, in your present condition, I don't want anything from you. But you were wrong in writing that you did not take any property with you.[2] I have none either, and it is possible that nobody among us will have any. I don't get any benefit out of it. If I want a bushel of corn, and if I take it from father, I pay him like any other neighbor. And what can yet happen with father's farm, nobody knows. As I said, it is possible that no one among us will get anything. . . . We might perhaps be able to prevent it, but we should think about it all together, because it is high time. . . .

W. Wróblewski

1. Walery probably asked for the payment of some money which Antoni owed him.

2. Wrong because it looked like a hint that Walery was profiting from the common family property.

October 7, 1907

DEAR BROTHER: .... Now as to our father, you wrote that Kostuś advises him to come to America, where he could quietly spend the rest of his age with him. This won't be. Although I have not spoken with father about it, I know that he would not go. And why should he? If he did not want to work himself on his farm, we could give him support but how can he part with his farm, leave the barn, etc.?[1] And Kostuś deserves praise for having taken care of you, but he might work himself in as dangerous a place, and if—God forbid!—any accident happened to him, with father in America, what then? It would be very unwise. And we could then give no effective help, because if we sent 10 roubles, you would receive there only 5, and moreover it is so difficult to get money here, while from America, when you send 5, we receive here 10, and that is a different thing. . . .

W. WRÓBLEWSKI

1. Ironical, meaning that he is too avaricious and egotistic to leave his property.

November 10, 1907

DEAR BROTHERS: .... Now I pass to the news. I inform you that our dear father [ironical] got married for the third time. He took for wife that Klimusia, or rather Franciszkowa [widow of Franciszek] Pilat, that bitch, so to speak, because she came in order to rob us. Her children did not drive her away from their home, but she wants to profit out of our fortune. When father gave [money] for the banns, he did not mention anything to us, but did it secretly. When we heard the banns of our father, we went directly to him with Józef, and we tried to persuade him in different ways not to marry. But he refused to listen, he wanted only to marry. We tried also to persuade her not to marry our father. About this time somebody broke her windows on All Saints' Day, and she throws the suspicion upon me; she had the policeman come and drew up a verbal process, and there will be a law suit. I will write you how this ends; but she has no witnesses to testify who broke her windows.[1] I also begged our priest to dissuade father from marrying her, but even this did not help, because the old man stubbornly stood upon marrying her. On Wednesday, November 6, the wedding was performed. We did not know anything about it, but I saw the old man coming back from the church, and I guessed it. On the very next day we went with Józef to say good morning to the new couple and we greeted them so that it went to their heels [proverbial: They felt it deeply.]. The old man saw that he could not evade and promised to give us the small lots to cultivate, and to leave for himself the riverside and Uskowizna. So he got rid of us for this time, but "Promise is a child's toy"; we won't be satisfied with it, we will insist as strongly as we can that he do it black upon white [in writing], for us and for you also. We care not only about ourselves, but also about you, lest Klimusia get it. She is a cunning [avaricious] old woman, since she dared to go to marriage almost in the face of violence. I will tell you everything that happens. We want father to will us all, everything, and to keep to it, but we don't know how it will turn out. Of course, we except Feliks, because he has his part already. I wrote you that he was in Jabłonowo with his family and did not show his eyes among us. He was there for 4 days and went back, although I know that he had leave for 2 weeks. That is also a meanness. What is the matter with our family, that they keep things secret from one another, like thieves?[2] . . .

W. WRÓBLEWSKI

1. Certainly the writer or his children did it.

2. Expression of the feeling that the family is disintegrating. "Keeping things secret" is clearly a proof that there is no real solidarity. In the primitive peasant family no member can have any secret from other members; there are no purely personal matters.

March 25, 1908

DEAR BROTHERS: . . . . I did not write, as I was waiting for the news which I expected from our father. We have called upon him more than once, with Józef, asking him to make some division of the farm, but he got stubborn and refuses to do anything for us; only to his Klimusia he refuses nothing. We called upon him with the priest, then alone, then with people; nothing helps.[1] Once he took an ax to us and tried to frighten us; he jumped around wildly, like a madman. He gives us in words the field in Szalajdy to sow, but Józef refuses to take it without a [written] will. I intend myself to harvest what I have sown, but I don't know how it will be later. Józef advises me not to do even this, but it seems to me that would be bad, for father will justify himself afterwards saying that he gave, but we would not take, and he will sell more readily. We also drove the Trusie [the stepmother's family] away from father's house, for they had settled their whole family already. Now at least they only call often. There would be much to write, whole newspapers would be necessary; in this letter the rest cannot be described. I spit upon all this, so to speak; if he is determined to waste all this, let him waste it; if his own children are not dear to him, only strange children, for everything there is free to strangers.

At the end of the carnival Józef Łaba got his daughter married to the son of Fortus from Łynki. We were not at the wedding, but father with his Klimusia was there, and he got so drunk that he lay under the hedge. The next day he invited perhaps half the people from Goździki, but we were left out. Although I never overlooked father [in my invitations], he always keeps away from us, as from enemies. Well, I end it, because I loathe all this.

W. W.

1. Calling with the priest and with people proves that in the general opinion the father is morally wrong in his behavior, that he ought to occupy the familial, not the personal standpoint.

February 22, 1910

DEAR BROTHERS: . . . . Now you asked me, dear brother, to write about our father. I can say that, although we don't live far from each other, I don't know anything about him, for he never comes to us and we never go to him. Why should we go, since he has disowned us. He said that he did not want our tutorship, that he will get on pretty well. It is true that he gets on pretty well, because from time to time we hear that he has sold some gully or patch. He keeps Klimusia and her children; they are all there continually, so we have no reason to go there. It is sad. But what can be done? I am happy only when I don't remember him, then my heart does not pain me. But whenever I recall it all I am very sad. If he were a father loving his own children and not those of others surely we should all be better off now. It is all right when strange brats [*bachory*, contemptful word for "children"] creep upon him from all sides like vermin, but he refused to live with his own children. I am not of his age today [it is natural for *old* people to live dependent on their children] but I live with my children upon their fortune, and still I don't weep. I commend myself to God's care and I live along. For me in my actual situation it is very bad that he did so, but may God's will be done. [Asks about the exact place of the brothers' farm upon the map, about the corn, vegetables, trees which grow there.] In our village and neighborhood a great deal is changed, it would seem strange to you now. And as to Feliks, I don't know for certain his address, because he does not write to us at all. . . . .

W. W.

Tuesday, December 10, 1907

DEAR BROTHER: . . . . I thank you for your letter, which pleased and grieved me at the same time. It pleased me because I learned something about you from your own hand, and grieved me because you described truly your situation. I knew about it long ago, it is true, but up to the last moment I could not believe that the danger was so imminent. How can I help you? I may only say that if you are unhappy (in this life), think that perhaps there are others, a hundred times more unhappy than you; and even those who at first sight seem to succeed well enough, if we looked nearer, and if we could discover the mysteries of their life, we should know that the life of every one of them is one series of sufferings. And if a man could see all his sufferings at once, he would certainly try to shorten them voluntarily.

But let us not talk about other people, only about ourselves. Let us begin with the oldest. Is Walery happy? Is everything with him going on as he wishes? At first it would seem we could say yes. It is but enough to look at the health of his wife and his children, particularly in their first years, in order to have an idea of his success. Further, was Marysia, in the flower of her age, happy? Certainly not. About Feliks I don't know much. But if somebody ordered me to be in his skin, a scapegoat, then I should be glad if there were ten Americas. You think probably that I make suppositions—true or not—about his wife. Then come you, I and Konstanty. We know about you. As to me, we can shrug our shoulders. To live alone seemed to me no business. I considered marriage a difficult duty, but nobody who has not experienced it can have any idea about it.

It is not because I have made a bad choice, but because with marriage are connected the most painful and irritating questions. I don't say that my condition is the worst, but it is far from being good, and the skies, instead of brightening, get clouded. Let us mention only one, the least important question. Every beast has its lair, the dog has his kennel, while we must wander about strange corners and depend upon the landlord's caprice, and we cannot even dream about our own kennel. And it is useless to speak about the rest. There remains Konstanty. I don't know how he succeeds. You write that he does very well, but I cannot believe that a man condemned to live far away from his native country could feel really happy.[1]

I was astonished in reading in your last letter the question, whether I had not forgotten you. In my opinion to forget for a long time one's brothers and sisters would be equal to forgetting for a long time to eat. Particularly now, when our father has disowned us, when our own father tries to harm us in every possible way—as you know probably from our brother's letters—we ought to be, all of us, near one another, "one for all and all for one." And if we cannot unify ourselves materially, then at least let us be united spiritually as closely as possible, and then it will be easier to bear the burden of life, and our Lord God will help us.[2]

[JÓZEF WRÓBLEWSKI]

1. The letter is full of meaning, showing the nature of the peasant's pessimism.
2. A good expression of the peasant's own conception of familial solidarity.

MARKIEWICZ SERIES

The Markiewiczs are a family of peasant nobility living in the province of Warsaw, near the Vistula and on the border of the province of Płock, but not like the Wróblewskis in their ancient family nest. This part of the country has almost no industry, but the neighborhood in which the family lives is not isolated from cultural influ-

1:455–57, 466–69, 507–13.

ence, as the town of Płock, lying across the river, is the seat of a rather strong intellectual movement. Life is much faster in this social environment that in that of the Wróblewskis, who come from the same class, and this may explain the difference of attitudes. Unlike Walery Wróblewski, the Markiewiczs are "climbers." The whole familial situation, the difference between the old and the young generation, and the individual differences of character and aspirations are much better understood if this fundamental feature is kept in mind. We find analogous situations in other familial series, but nowhere so universally and fully presented in its most interesting stage, i.e., at the moment when the tendency to rise *within* their own class begins to change into a tendency to rise *above* their own class. The situation of the family Markiewicz is thus representative of the general situation of the middle and lower classes of Polish society. It is a family in which the characters of the old society, with its fixed classes of families, and the new society, with its fluid classes of individuals, are mixed together in various proportions. . . . The two older brothers, Józef and Jan, are typical peasants whose sphere of interests is completely enclosed within the old social group. They do not tend to rise above their class, and they do not understand the conscious or unconscious tendencies of their children in this direction. Each of them wants his family to occupy the highest possible place within the community—his family as a whole, not one or another individual in particular, not even his own personality, which he does not dissociate from that of his family. All the efforts of Józef and Jan are concentrated upon this aim. They both economize as much as possible, making little distinction between their own money and that of their children; they both buy land wherever there is any opportunity; they try to profit from every source of income; they neglect any showing off except in the traditional lines, giving no money to dress their children, but spending large sums on wedding festivals. They endow their children very well but want them to make good matches. They give their children instruction but only as far as instruction helps to attain a higher standing in the community itself, and provided it does not lead to ideas contrary to the traditions. They do not understand at first how their sons in America can have any other aim than to gather as much money as possible in order to come back and buy good farms and marry rich peasant girls. When they begin to understand that their sons' sphere of interests has become different from their own, the discovery leads either to a tragic appeal or to a more or less complete estrangement between father and son.

THE FAMILY MARKIEWICZ

Józef Markiewicz
Anna, his wife
Wacław (Wacio, Wacek), their son
Jan Markiewicz, Józef's brother
His wife
Maks (Maksymilian), their son

The first group of letters are from Józef and Anna to their son Wacław in the United States. Wacław has abandoned religion and has become a socialist.

February 24, 1908

DEAR SON: We received your letter. . . . We wish you to be healthy in body and soul, because this is the excellence of man. For the second year is passing already, and you don't mention anything about religion or church. Remember the admonition of your parents. For faith is the first thing, and everything else is only additional. Don't step aside from the true way. Consider it, for you can do harm to your whole family.[1]

And now I inform you that rye is 7 roubles [a bushel]. Thanks to God there is work in the windmill; the barn brings also a few bushels [for space rented?] and so we try as best we can that there may be more and more [property] for you [children].

Dear son, reflect well, if you are working beyond the ocean only for the sake of living [without saving], leave it and come to us.[2] If you have a few hundred roubles, I will take [add] my money, and I will buy a farm somewhere for you. The inn in Dobrzyków is now for sale, or perhaps something else. . . .

JÓZEF MARKIEWICZ

1. Probable meaning: "God may punish the whole family for your sins." Thus, the feeling of familial unity is carried so far as to acknowledge a common responsibility before God.

2. The new tendency to advance as against the old interest in mere living is here expressed as clearly as possible. Fifty years ago it was all right if a young member of a family, which was too poor to support all its members, earned his living by servant work and thus spared the rest of the family his living expenses; there was not even the idea of his increasing the familial fortune, for he had no wages in cash. . . . But here, with regard to Wacław, the situation of the family is almost brilliant when measured by peasant standards, and still Wacław should increase the fortune. If he cannot do it by working in America he ought to do it by farmer's work. If he does nothing but live on his income he is regarded as losing his time.

March 29, 1908

DEAR SON: I received your letter. I rejoiced much that you are in good health, but for another cause you make us sad, for you don't intend to come back to our country. At this moment the paper trembled in my hand or my hand shook in recording it. Why, even birds who fly away from their native place still do come back! How did you dare to pronounce such wretched [mean] words? You ought to hold to the parental exhortations. I never taught you to criticize the clergy. You know that Bonaparte shook the whole of Europe until he broke off with the head of the Church, and later—you know what became of him later! Well, I don't mention that you forgot about religion, i.e., about the greatest jewel, only that after a year you [raise yourself?] above us. What you give to the papers is bad, and it is a pity that you use your learning so, for learning is everywhere useful to man, but [your ideas] are useful to you there, but won't be when you come back. . . .

And now with us it is as it has been. . . . As to money, we don't absolutely require you to send any when you cannot, because I try always to have a few hundred roubles on hand. Only don't forget about yourself for your later years. . . .

J. MARKIEWICZ

Dear son, why are you so angry and why do you answer us so severely? The girls wept after reading this letter, so that it was quite gloomy in the house. And we, the parents, what are we to say? You don't want to come back to us, but I don't think it true. I believe in you that you love your parents and your country. . . .

[YOUR MOTHER]

September 7, 1909

DEAR SON: . . . . And as to the letters from you, we had none except last year in July for my name-day. Then we answered at once and we asked you for an answer, but we received no letter until to-day, September 7. Dear son, believe us, there was not a day when we did not complain about your negligence, and you complain about us! Neither letter nor postcard, nothing up to the present. I don't know what happened. We have only this letter which you tell us to send to the editor [of some paper]. As for me, I fall asleep with the thought about you and I awake with the same thought; I end the day with tears and I begin it with tears. I did not understand what happened to you. Everybody at home tried to comfort me, but it was hard to wait. Your father went to Jan M[arkiewicz] in order that he might ask Maks. They said that Maks wrote about your having gone somewhere without giving any word of yourself, but they did not allow us to read the letter.

With us everything is as it has been from old; we have a horse, worth 100 roubles, a new wagon, 3 cows, 2 calves, 4 pigs worth also about 100 [roubles], etc. The crops are the average. Franuś [son-in-law] is captain [of a Vistula boat]. They bought 6 morgs of land. We have given them some money already, but we will add some more, for we must give them at least 500 roubles. Teosia and Wacek were with us for a week, but they did not say anything about the loan, so it is probably a lie. We heard that they said something to Franuś. They are all worth the same [little]. Well, God be with them. I don't see any blessing of God for them.[1] They had only her [one daughter] and even so they came to us asking for a hundred [roubles] for her wedding. . . .

Your father was in Włocławek. . . . and called upon Edek. Edek said that he saw you in the spring and that you intend to come back to our country. If you think it good, then come. He said that you are some sort of a boss, and that you earn about $400. Can it be? Or perhaps it is only a slander of your enemies; I don't know. Your grandmother began to reproach us for your education, saying that we have praised you so much, and now you don't write. We grieve ourselves enough. All other people do write, and we don't have any news. How hard and painful it is when anybody asks us [about you]. We were quite ashamed at last. . . .

[MARKIEWICZS]

1. We see how success may assume a moral value by being conceived as the result of God's blessing. Formally this conception was introduced by the church in its endeavor to ascribe to God all the good. But the content is really older. Prosperity was a sign of a harmony between man and nature.

The second group of letters is from Maks in America to his cousin Wacław. Maks has little of the peasant even in the beginning of his career in America, and almost nothing after seven years spent in this country. He drops all the peasant ideals one after another—agriculture, property, communal interests, and familial solidarity (without losing attachment to individual members of the family)—and, while keeping the climbing tendencies of his father, develops them along a new line, in the typical middle-class career.

SOUTH CHICAGO, August 7, 1906

DEAR BROTHER WACŁAW [really cousin]: Fortune arranged it so that unexpectedly we both became pilgrims in America. So I feel my brotherly attachment to you, and that it is so, let it be proved by my letter addressed to you, whose address I got from home.[1] I dare say that perhaps you care less to establish a regular correspondence with me here in America, but it is only a supposition. How it is in reality the future will show.

So I inform you that I came to America, i.e., to New York, on February 13, and then I went to my friends in New Kensington. . . . There I worked up to May 26. I worked in a glass factory 8 hours a day. The work was not heavy, but hot. I earned $12.50 to $14.00 a week; it depended on how much glass was made.

I left because the factory closed. . . . I went to Chicago. There I found my acquaintances and my cousin Leonard Król, my mother's uncle's son, with whom I am living up to the present. Since I came to South Chicago, I am working with Polish carpenters 8 hours a day. I am paid 35¢ an hour. And naturally, while it is summer, I am very busy with this work, but in winter it will surely stop. Then I hope to get into a factory . . . or carshop for the same work. On the 2d of this month I received a letter from home, favorable enough, and at the same time your address. So I want to learn about you, what you are doing, where and with whom you live. And in general inform me about your success. Whatever you ask me, I will gladly inform you about. . . . I send you hearty wishes of happiness, health and good success, I embrace you and kiss you. Your brother,

MAKSYMILIAN [MAKS MARKIEWICZ]

1. Typical, disinterested revival of family feelings. It is not merely the result of loneliness, for Maks lives with another cousin.

March 27, 1907

DEAR BROTHER: Your letter satisfied me very much, for you have good work. I remember the letter which you wrote to me last summer; I pitied you then, when you described how you worked in a glass factory for $1.50 a day. My hearty advice to you would be to hold steadily to carpenter's work, particularly in carshops, for though they pay better in other works, it is not so steady as in a carshop. Moreover, if you know how to work about cars you can find this work in the whole of America. I intend also in the future to get into a passenger carshop, for not far from me there is a big carshop in which thousands of carpenters are working. It is, I have heard, the main carshop for whole America, called "Pullman." From there come the most splendid cars for all lines. Look carefully, then you will surely see these cars with the inscription "Pullman."

When Stasio comes, if there is nothing favorable for him where you are, let him come to me, then I will help him as much as I can. But you know that a man who comes fresh from our country can [only] with difficulty find good work, for he is not acquainted with the American habits and does not understand the language. Therefore I warn you, let Stasio not be very capricious in the beginning. I wish [advise] him also to try carpenter's work.[1] . . .

MAKSYMILIAN

1. The problem of work, predominant in this letter and important in all the letters of American Poles, plays no such role in the life of the Polish peasant farmer. With him work, that is work for others, is only an additional means of existence, and property is his main interest. There is in the old country no hope of advance through work. It is undertaken only as a means of supplementing an otherwise impossible existence, and is miserably paid. In this respect American emigration, with its many possibilities and its relatively vast range of good and bad chances, effects a profound revolution in the psychology of the peasant, and the problem of work becomes at once the central problem. Interests of the city workman are added to those of the peasant, without supplanting them, and the result is that the workman of peasant

origin differs from the hereditary city workman in two respects: (1) He has no interest in the work itself but considers it exclusively with regard to the wage; (2) he looks upon his labor, not as a means of organizing his life once and forever, but as a provisional state, a means of attaining property, which is for him the only possible basis of a steady life organization. The good job, particularly in America, is for the peasant nothing but a good chance from which he must get as much as possible, while for a man with a workman's psychology and with the same tendency to rise the good job will be either an end in itself or a means of getting a still better job. From this results also the apparent stinginess and low standard of life with which the American workman reproaches the Polish immigrant. The man with a workman's psychology, considering hired work as his more or less permanent condition, will try to live as comfortably and pleasantly as his means permits, for this life is normal for him. The man with the peasant psychology, considering hired work as a temporary chance, will reduce his actual needs to a minimum, postponing every pleasure of life until the end of his work, for this life is for him provisional and abnormal. The letters of Maks give us a good example of the evolution of this attitude. In the beginning Maks is an instructed peasant, economizing, putting money aside, thinking of returning, and probably of acquiring some property at home. Then he hesitates and is half-decided not to return; he is not yet decided to remain a workman, but he already has expenses which only a workman, never a peasant, would make, such as buying a watch for $60. He nevertheless still thinks of property and writes about buying a house. And, finally, he does something which is absolutely contrary to peasant psychology; he decides to spend all his money on instruction and goes to a college. This proves that no longer property but hired work has become his life business and that his peasant attitude in economic matters has changed into a typical workman's attitude.

September 5, 1907

DEAR BROTHER: . . . . I see that you did not receive my last letter . . . and you probably think that I have forgotten you. But in this respect you are mistaken, dear brother, for I don't intend ever to forget anybody, and particularly you. As to your supposition that some woman turned my head, you almost guessed it. But I know also how to turn women's heads. Only I keep always in mind the severe American laws in this regard.[1] [Was slightly hurt in his left hand; expects to get insurance money.]

MAKSYMILIAN

1. The attitude of Maks toward the problem of love is already to some extent that of the middle class. In the peasant class love is always related to marriage, even if there is much flirting before making the definite choice; in the middle class it becomes an end in itself, a kind of sport, of which marriage in each given case

may be the result, but is not necessarily the acknowledged aim. Of course, as sexual intercourse between unmarried people is normally excluded in the middle class, there must be a sufficient degree of culture in order to make the relation interesting in spite of this limitation and in spite of the lack of an immediate reference to marriage, and it is also usually possible only when the individual is no longer dependent upon the family.

INDIANA HARBOR, April 30, 1908

DEAR BROTHER WACŁAW: . . . . I inform you that I moved from South Chicago to Indiana Harbor, nearer my work, so that now I can go on foot to the factory and I don't need to pay 15¢ a day for the railway passage.[1]

I was much pleased with your intention to learn English, and even higher [subjects], for if you have some instruction, you will have an assured existence in this country. I guess that you regret that you did not come to America a few years sooner [before his military service], and did not learn English instead of learning Russian [in the army], you could say today boldly that your existence is secure.[2]

I got a letter also from our country, from father, mother, and brother Wiktor. When Wiktor was still in Petersburg I wrote him that I intended to marry in America, and that I would therefore never come back to our country. I asked him to repeat to my parents my decision wholly [as I wrote it], but, instead of sending it by letter, he told it himself to my parents when he came back home. This is what he wrote me, that he was able to notice: My mother was very much troubled about it and began to cry, longing for me, while my father cared about it very little, and Wiktor noticed that father cared little about it. Then, my mother begs me much, in her first letter to me, to remove these thoughts from my head, to come back to our country, while my father does not mention a word about my returning home, only informs me with joy, that Wiktor came back healthy from the army. And when Wiktor was to draw the lot, my father, as I heard, exerted himself [to get him free], and even gave to some official 200 roubles to this effect, so that if the commission in Gostynin exempted Wiktor from the military service, it would cost my father 200 roubles, but if not, then the official would pay the money back. Well, the commission did not exempt him, and my father got the money back. Therefore he writes me now [when Wiktor, because of bad health, has been sent back from the army], that Wiktor is there and the money is there. From [in spite of] his joy, as my brother writes me, father would not even buy him clothes for Easter. In a word, dear brother, I don't see in my father any heart for me, now no more than formerly.[3] At the same time I got a letter from my mother, written with her own hand. She weeps for me and she asks me with tears to come back to our country. My heart grieves at the words of my beloved mother, and I am ready to satisfy her wish in the future.

As to the question how I look upon religion and socialism, dear brother, I don't bother myself profoundly with either the first or the second. Not with the former, because I know this much, that I am a Catholic, and I perform the duties of a Catholic as far as I can. I am not devout, for I have no time to pray, because every Sunday I must work, and—I confess it to you alone—I worked even on Easter from 7 until 2. . . . But nevertheless I desire to remain a Catholic up to my death.

As to politics, I am very little interested in any questions or parties; when I have a little time, I buy a paper for 1¢. I read it, and there it all ends.[4] . . .

M. MARKIEWICZ

1. He had lived for a year as described in order to be with a remote cousin.

2. We find here already a standpoint very different from that of the peasant tradition. The question of "existence" is put upon a purely individual basis. But this standpoint is not yet definitely accepted, as the following paragraph shows.

3. Maks evidently had his father sounded with reference to determining what were his chances of receiving the farm or of being established on another if he returned, and the uncordial attitude of his father perhaps had an effect in determining the individualistic sentiments in the earlier part of the letter.

4. In comparison with Maks, Wacław remains more of a peasant, in spite of his socialism. Instruction is not for him a means of getting a position on a higher social level. He is enough above the peasant to appreciate instruction in itself, independent of its immediate practical application, but not enough to make of it a new basis of life. Economically he is satisfied to belong to the lower class and wants to rise only socially. Maks, on the contrary, is not interested in instruction and theoretical problems as a matter of distinction, but he gets further from the peasant ideology than Wacław and is able to make instruction a new life basis which will allow him to get totally outside of the peasant class economically as well as socially. Wacław expresses his desire to do the same as Maks, but it does not seem that he fulfilled it.

September 22, 1908

DEAR BROTHER: . . . . After waiting for 6 months, I received at last a letter from my father, with rather favorable news. . . . They are succeeding pretty well, for my father intends to buy in Dobrzyków the *murowanka* [farm with stone buildings] from Mr. Plebanek for 3,300 roubles, but he has not this whole sum, so he addressed himself to me for some help. I did not refuse him help in this affair, but it seems to me now that perhaps I acted impolitely. I asked my father to send me first notes for 1,000 roubles or more, and promised to send money at once after receiving these. (Tell me your opinion about this question of notes and sending money in general.) I add that if I asked for notes it was because my confidence in my father has been ruined during my stay in America. If you wish, I can tell you about it. . . .

M. MARKIEWICZ

December 14, 1908

DEAR BROTHER: I am very much grieved that you are in so bad a position. I can well imagine your painful situation, and I should be glad to help you, dear brother, and at the same time I would reach the object of my wishes to live together, or near each other in this foreign land. But now it is simply impossible. In the factory where I am working very few men have good work—only the engineers and we three carpenters. As to the ordinary workers in the mill, may God pity them, so bad is their work. . . . I would not wish it, not only not to my brother, but not even to the Russian [tsar] Nicholas to get it by my protection [assistance]. Perhaps in the future you will have occasion to see it yourself; then you will agree with me that I was right. . . . As to the carshops, they are not here, but near Chicago, but I hear that even they don't work with full speed, as the papers have drummed it after the election of Taft. If you want money, write to me and I will send you some.[1] . . . With me everything is good. I am healthy, I work steadily, only I am bored here, because in this small town I am as solitary as in a forest. . . . Write me what do you think about the Polish National Alliance and the Polish Sokols. . . .

M. MARKIEWICZ

1. He kept this promise, but without taking money from the bank.

August 16, 1909

DEAR BROTHER WACŁAW: . . . . I received a good letter from my parents, and besides the letter I received beautiful gifts from my parents, brought by Witkowski's brother—a gold watch chain, my monogram sewed with gold and silver threads and six fine handkerchiefs, marked. I am very much pleased with these tokens, and from joy I bought a gold watch for $60.00. I won't write you more, for I intend . . . to come to you next Sunday. . . .

MAKSYMILIAN

October 5, 1909

DEAR BROTHER WACŁAW: . . . . I inform you about an offer from which you will perhaps profit. My old boss told me today that he had much work, so perhaps I knew some carpenters, and if so I should send them to him. I told him that I had a brother carpenter (i.e., you) who was working, but if the work would be steady, I could bring him. He answered that he hoped to have steady work. So I advise you to come, dear brother . . . we would live here in the foreign land together. . . . We could meet him in South Chicago and speak about the business while drinking a glass of beer. . . .

MAKS

ISLAND CITY, November 18, 1911

DEAR BROTHER: . . . . I am glad to hear that you want to send me your money for keeping. I see that you smother [hoard] it well. So send it and don't ask whether I will accept it. Describe how long the work there can last, what are you building, and how do you live there. I think there are probably colds and snows. . . . Take care not to catch cold and not to journey thence [into the other world]. Write more about yourself and the country. Are you satisfied with your success? With me there is no news. . . .

M.

Raczkowski Series

These letters show, in a very detailed and varied manner, the influence of emigration upon family life. We see that every individual undergoes a different evolution, but that there are always factors explaining these differences.

In general emigration, as should be expected, by isolating the individual from the family and from the community, provokes individualization and weakens the control of the primary group; we have found it already in some of the preceding series. But the degrees and varieties of individualization are numerous.

[Adam Raczkowski] adapted himself rapidly to American life and succeeded without difficulty in attaining a material position, which, when measured by the peasant standard, must have seemed to him almost brilliant. He gradually ceases to consider it his duty to help his family, but he does not break the familial ties and occasionally—partly from generosity, partly from the desire to manifest his personal importance—responds to the appeals of other members.

His case illustrates the effect of economic conditions on the expansion and development of the personality. Economic success is one of the main sources of the feeling of personal importance, and therefore this feeling is found almost universally among American immigrants. It develops also in Poland under the same influence. . . . But, generally speaking, the feeling of personal importance can never develop so rapidly and to such a degree under the influence of a merely economic progress in Poland as it does in America; it is hindered by many social traditions. The social standing of the peasant within the community cannot rise very much through his economic progress if his family does not progress economically at the same time. This limitation partly disappears with the dissolution of the old family, but another tradition is incomparably more difficult for an individual to rid himself of—the old hierarchy of classes. This is more and more supplanted by the new social orga-

---

2:180–92, 194–96, 202–3, 206, 211–12, 217–23. In the unabridged work, this family has significantly more members than appear here.

nization on the basis of the middle-class principle, but it still has strength enough to make an individual of the lower class feel at every moment his social inferiority through the infinitely numerous and various details in which the principle of hierarchy has expressed itself during the many centuries of its dominance.

Finally, even within the new social organization mere economic progress is not sufficient to give the individual the full feeling of personal importance, because the new hierarchy is not exclusively based upon economic differences, but, even more, upon differences of intellectual culture.

Now in America these obstacles do not exist, at least not to such an extent. The individual is isolated almost completely from the family group. The traditional class distinctions, even if they exist, are neither old nor important enough to make themselves felt by the lower classes. The new class organization is based mainly upon economic differences, and thus economic progress seems the only test of individual value. The cultural criteria are developed in particular groups but do not pervade the society as a whole. Finally, the immigrant has, as a background for his own personality, not only American life but the life in the old country, and it is the comparison with his own previous condition and the condition of his people at home which makes him feel his personal importance in so strong and exaggerated a way.

Another important problem raised in this series is the relation between parents and children among Polish immigrants in America. The state of things about which Helena complains in her letters—the impossibility of controlling the children—is very general, and is probably more serious among the Poles than any other nationality. While the external factors of emancipation are the same for the children of every race, we must understand exactly the social conditions which make the Poles react differently to these factors. To be sure, the problem is how far the parents will be able to oppose their authority to the disintegrating influences of the environment, and this depends upon the adaptation of the means of control to the circumstances. In Polish peasant life this adaptation is sufficient. We have seen . . . that the parental authority finds there its foundation in the whole organization of the family and in the social opinion of the community; the family and the community have a sufficient power of sanction to prevent any revolt of the child and at the same time to hold the parents responsible for any abuse. The parental authority in the eyes of the children seems not only sacred and all-powerful, but also just and raised above individual caprice.

If we contrast now the conditions at home with those which the emigrants meet in America, we see that a loss of control over the child is inevitable if the parents do not develop new means as substitutes for the old ones. First, there is in America no family in the traditional sense; the married couple and the children are almost completely isolated, and the parental authority has no background. (In a few cases, where many members of the family have settled in the same locality, the control is much stronger.) Again, if there is something equivalent to the community of the old country, i.e., the parish, it is much less closed and concentrated and can hardly have the same influence. Its composition is new, accidental, and changing; moreover, it is composed of various elements, each influenced separately and each somewhat differently by the new environment, and has consequently a rather poor stock of common traditions. Further, the members of the new generation, brought up in this new environment, are more likely to show a solidarity with one another as against the parents than a solidarity with the parents as against the younger members of the family. Finally, economic independence comes much earlier than in the old country and makes a revolt always materially easy. On the other hand, the parents' authority ceases also to be controlled, except by the state in the relatively rare cases of a far-going abuse. The traditional measure of its exertion is lost; the parents have no standard of education, since the old social standard is no longer valid and no new one has been appropriated. The natural result is a free play given to individual caprice, excessive indulgence alternating with unreasonable severity. Thus the moral character of parental authority in the eyes of the children is lost.

The immigrant can therefore control his children only if he is able to substitute individual authority for social authority and to base his influence, not upon his position as representative of the group, but upon his personal superiority. But this, of course, requires a higher degree of individual culture, intellectual and moral, than most of the immigrants can muster. The contrary case is more frequent, where the children assume a real or imagined superiority to the parents on account of their higher instruction and their better acquaintance with American ways, etc.

The same problems confront country people moving to a Polish town; there, however, the break in the social control of family life is neither so rapid nor so complete, the change of the young generation is not so radical, and there are often time and opportunity enough to substitute a sufficient amount of individual authority for the lost part of social authority.

THE FAMILY RACZKOWSKI

Raczkowski, a retired farmer
Wawrzonkowa, his second wife
Franciszek } his sons
Adam
Helena } his daughters
Teofila

WILMINGTON, DEL., June 24 [1904]

DEAR SISTER: .... I am already with my brother, thanks to God and to God's Mother. As to work, I don't hope to work sooner than autumn, because brother also has no work since Christmas and cannot get work, because all factories are stopped and there is no work until they elect the president in autumn. Then perhaps we shall get work. And at present brother has no pleasure in life either, because there are five of them and I make the sixth, and all this means spending money. And you know that when I left you, I had neither clothes nor shirts; so when I came to them, sister-in-law and brother gave me at once clothes of theirs and we all three went to the city and bought clothes, one suit for working days and another for holidays, and everything in the way of clothes. So you can understand that when we bought everything, it cost them about 80 roubles. The watch and the suit for church cost alone 60 roubles.[1] I have nothing more to write, only I bid you goodbye, dear sister and brother-in-law. When I get work I won't forget you. Remain with God. Both Raczkowskis with their children send also their bows. I beg you, answer the soonest possible.

[ADAM RACZKOWSKI]

1. Franciszek R. and Helena Brylska have divided between themselves the expense burden of bringing Adam to America. Helena paid for the ship ticket, Franciszek supports Adam until he gets work. This is still familial solidarity.

September 23, 1904

DEAR SISTER: . . . . I received your letter and I thank you heartily for answering me. As to what you write, sister, that I may greet Brylska [i.e., Helena] for you, well, I wrote her three letters and she wrote me one and sent us her photograph when she got married. As soon as I came to America, I saluted her politely. But brother and sister-in-law related to me how she remembered [forgot] her children and how she began to behave as soon as she came to America. And she complained to us that sister-in-law was not good to her! She behaved so that if it had been I, I should not have kept her [in the house] 24 hours. As it was, they were patient and kept her, and brother tried to find work for her. And about her writing letters to Wawrzonkowa [their stepmother] and sending money to her, well, I shall bow to her [to Brylska] more profoundly [I will despise her for it still more] because if Wawrzonkowa were lying under a hedge and if I were passing by, I would—kick her, but would not give my hand to her [assist her].[1] [Usual greetings.]

ADAM RACZKOWSKI

1. Adam's behavior toward his sister who had helped him to come to America and had done him no personal wrong seems to be mean ingratitude and would be this if their relation had been merely personal. But Adam evidently occupies not the individual but the familial standpoint. He condemns Brylska impersonally for her alleged lack of familial feelings toward her own children, toward Franciszek and his wife, and from this standpoint the act of solidarity in sending Adam a ship ticket cannot counterbalance those alleged offenses against the spirit of the family. The familial standpoint becomes still more marked when Adam reproaches Helena for her solidarity with Wawrzonkowa, the stepmother. The latter is for him not only not a member of the family but an element hostile to the family.

February 13 [1905]

DEAR SISTER: . . . . And now I inform you that I have very good work. I have been working for 3 months. I have very good and easy work. I earn $8.00 a week. Brother has work also. And as to Brylska, I don't know how she is getting on, and I don't think about her at all. Inform me what is going on in our country, who has come to America, and who got married, and what is the talk in our country about revolution and war, because I have paid for a newspaper for a whole year and the paper comes to me twice a week[1] so they write that in our country there is misery. They say in Warsaw and Petersburg there is a terrible revolution and many people have perished already. As to the money, I cannot help you now, sister. You will excuse me yourself; I did not work for five months. . . .

ADAM RACZKOWSKI

1. This mention, trifling in itself, is a significant expression of the multiplication of contacts which will result in a more and more intense feeling in the man of his own personality, as we shall see in his later letters.

June 27, 1906

DEAR SISTER: . . . . As to the work, I am working in the same factory, and brother also is working in the same factory, where he was working formerly. And as to our country, brother says he will not return, because there is nothing to return for. He has no property there, and it is better for him in America, because in our country he could not even earn enough for a loaf of bread. And I also do not know whether I shall return or not. If I can return then perhaps I shall return some day or other, and if not I don't mind, because I do ten times better in America than in our country. I do better today than brother, because I am alone. As to Borkowianka,[1] I don't know whether she came to America or not, because I sent her neither a ship ticket nor money. So I beg you, sister, be so kind and learn from the Borkowskis whether she thinks of coming or not, because if she does not come then I will marry in the autumn or during carnival.[2]

1. A woman friend.
2. There is not question of love. Probably under the influence of his sister he is thinking of Borkowianka. He simply wants to marry in general.

January 28, 1907

DEAR SISTER: . . . . As to work, I work, but very little, because the factory where we worked with brother was burned on Saturday, January 19, at 7 o'clock in the evening, and brother's carpenter's tools were all burned. He lost $50.00. And now I inform you about my old Miss Borkowska, whom nobody wants. I don't care anything about her—such an old maid! I wrote to her only in jest, because I have in America girls enough and much better than she, and even to them I don't pay compliments. I care as much for her as for an old torn shoe. Today I don't need the favor of anybody except God. May God continue to give me such health as he gives me up to the present day. I don't want the favors of anybody except God. As to Teofil, I don't know what he means, and why he will take to himself such a shepherd's bitch. There is no place in America for her, because in America they don't keep sheep. Does he want to keep sheep, and to breed rams, and to become a shepherd? The stupid, where is his reason, since in America there are girls enough.[1]

As to money, I won't send you any now, because we have expenses ourselves, but I will send you for the holidays some more roubles; you may expect it. . . .

1. This abuse is evidently the effect of resentment, particularly as the girl seems to have shown a preference for Teofil. (Borkowska is another name for the Borkowianka whom he has previously mentioned.) But it shows mainly the degree of self-conceit which the man has already reached. The feeling of personal importance and exaltation, based on economic success, is here mixed with a feeling of independence, whose source lies probably in the progressive liberation from the bonds of social tradition, including family and traditional attitudes toward marriage, power of the community, and probably also power of the state, which he had experienced during military service.

[June?] 3, 1907

DEAR SISTER: . . . . As to the work, brother is working steadily and since the factory was burned I have had work for a month and for another month I have had no work. During the two years I worked steadily in the same factory I had money, and now I earn hardly enough to live. I am working in the same factory as brother. I do carpenter's work and earn $2.00 a day. The work is good and well paid, but only if you work steadily. May God let me work this year during the summer in that factory and earn at least enough to live. Then by winter I shall have steady work.

This letter, which I received from you, grieved me and brother terribly. Dear sister and brother-in-law, you write to us to hold our hands out to you [help you]. It is true that a misfortune befell you, that a misery from God happened to you, and you have not a piece of bread to put in your mouth at times, but with us also it is not easy. Before we earn that cent in the sweat of our brow and get it into our hands, see here, an expense is waiting for it. I don't need to explain everything to you, because you know yourself what expenses are. But in such misfortune we will not refuse you, and not send you any money, but we will not send it now. We will send it to you on June 15, because we cannot do it sooner. I will not write to you how much until a second letter. . . .

Inform me, how are the crops in our country, and what success, and who got married among the young people, and whether my companions came back from the army or not. I leave you with respect and beg for a speedy answer.[1]

ADAM RACZKOWSKI

1. The whole tone of the letter shows a certain lowering of the feeling of personal importance, to be explained probably by (1) worse economic conditions and (2) a certain revival of old memories, which is shown by the interest manifested in the persons and conditions of the "old country," and which brings the man back to his earlier attitude.

January 24, 1907 [1908]

DEAR SISTER: . . . . I will tell you about myself, how I am doing in America. I have not yet experienced poverty in America; on the contrary, I am my brother's support. But I am tired of walking about unmarried. Although I could give my wife enough to live, still I fear lest poverty should look me in the eyes. Were it not for the money I have put in my brother's house, which he bought, I could do nothing during a year and live with my wife like a lord. But now I postpone it for a longer time. . . .

ADAM RACZKOWSKI

May God allow us to live till Easter, and after Easter I will write to you what girl I shall marry, and I will send you a photograph as soon as I leave the altar. My girl is a cousin of my sister-in-law; her mother and my sister-in-law are born sisters. They are persuading me to marry her, but I still doubt whether it will be so.

ADAM RAKOSKI [sic]

March 2, 1908

DEAR SISTER: . . . . As to Teofil I do not know where he is, because he was with me before Christmas and was out of work then, and he intended to go to the mines. So I don't know whether he went or not, because in mines it is this way: One goes there and finds money, another, death. He wanted to go to the mines, so probably he went, because he has not written to me. As to work, I haven't worked for four weeks. There is not work. Brother still works but is not doing well, because almost all factories are closed. Times are so good in America that people are going begging. As to sister, I don't know anything about her, because she does not write to me, and I do not write to her either.

You advise me to marry Księżakówna. Besides Księżakówna I have others [here] even more stately and I do not bestir myself very much about them.[1] As to Imnielsczanka [daughter of Imnielski], send her to me, and I will marry her and send you the money for the ship ticket back. Now is not a very good time to marry, because work is bad and bad times are coming now.

ADAM RACZKOWSKI

1. A curious example of an attitude remaining superficially the same while the social background is completely changed. As long as the boy is more a member of a family, the familial dignity requires him not to show too much eagerness in his courtship—to hesitate, really or apparently, to make his choice slowly and from among many girls. When the individual is isolated, we should expect an easier and more rapid decision and more place for personal preferences. And normally this is so. But here the feeling of personal importance takes the place of the demands of familial dignity, and the old behavior is kept up while its psychological factors are quite new.

February 25, 1910

DEAR SISTER: . . . . I received your letter on Christmas, but I did not answer you at once, because I intended to marry, and therefore I waited with the letter, even too long. Excuse me, dear sister and brother-in-law; don't be angry with me. At last I now inform you, that I am married. My wedding was on January 24. I have a wife from the government of Płock, from Sierpc, beyond Mława. And now we send you this letter and the wedding photograph. I am in this photograph and my wife. After Easter brother will send you also his own with his family. He will send you none now because his wife is not able to go to the photographer. I describe my wedding in another letter. At present I will mention only this, that this wedding cost me $180. The wedding dress alone cost me $30.00 and about the rings and other things I shall not write you. I took her as rich as she walked [having nothing]. I paid $85.00 back for her ship ticket. In another letter I will tell you everything that is going on in America, and everything in general. I have nothing more to write, only I send you my greetings. I embrace you and kiss you innumerable times, and my wife also salutes sister and brother-in-law, embraces and kisses sister and brother-in-law, and remains with respect, Zofia Raczkowska.

And I ask you for a speedy answer, when you receive the photograph.

ADAM RACZKOWSKI

November 28, [1912]

DEAR SISTER: You write to us and ask us to send you a ship ticket for your boy. We advise you to let him wait until spring, because it is not certain how work will be in the spring for now they have elected a democrat president and when a democrat is president everybody expects misery to come. Let him wait until March, because only from March on this president will begin to govern, and we shall see how work goes when he governs, whether well or ill. Now work is bad. Brother worked for 9 years in the same factory, and this year he has not worked since spring, because work is stopping. We neither advise you nor dissuade. Sister intends to send him a ship ticket.[1] . . . .

ADAM AND FRANCISZEK RACZKOWSKI

1. The personal feelings of women are never so completely subordinated to the forms of social solidarity as are those of the men, and on the disintegration of a family the individual affection of women is less likely to disappear than the group solidarity of the men.

UNION CITY, CONN. April 8 [1904]

DEAR SISTER: I am working in the same place where I was working, and I live nearer the factory, so my address will be different. I have sent you money, 20 roubles, and I have no word whether you received it or not. I don't know what it means. I have sent a ship

ticket for brother [Adam] and I don't know either what it means
that I have no word. Has he left already or not? What does it mean
that you don't answer me? Since Christmas I have no word from you.
What does it mean? Are you angry with me? I don't know what is
going on, whether you got angry, or you don't wish to write to me,
or perhaps the address is bad? I beg you, dear sister, inform me
about my children, because I think about them very much and I
long for them more than in the beginning, because here in America there are rumors that there is war in our country.[1] We know from
the papers; papers come every day and we know about everything.
Answer me, dear sister and brother-in-law, about your health and
success, tell me about everything, whether good or bad, because
brother now is far away from me, he went to his wife's family. The
ticket in one direction costs $7.00 and the second [brother], if he
left for America, I shall not see him either, because he had a ship
ticket bought to them.[2] Perhaps I shall go to them in about half a
year. . . .

HELENA BRYLSKA

1. The reason of the growing longing is probably not the one given. We see the
longing growing continually until the children come, without reference to any
question of war or any other cause of anxiety. In the beginning the relative novelty of the practical situation in which she found herself and the necessity of adapting herself to the new conditions left no place for remembrance and sentiment.
The more settled the situation becomes, the more normal the life and the greater the margin left for representation of the past and dreams of the future. And
we see from many examples that for the fundamentally practical peasant, recollection is essential to the arousing of a pure sentiment, and how much isolation
from the disturbances of practical life this recollection requires.

2. The longing is not only for the children, but for the family and the old country in general. She begins to feel lonely.

[No date]

DEAR SISTER: You ask me to send you money. I answer, that now
I can send none, because the factories are going bankrupt; it means
they are stopping work. So I fear that if I send money home and
the factories stop, I shall remain without work and without money.
I shall see later on; perhaps I shall send you some when work gets
better. I work in the same factory. And now I salute you, dear brother, and I request you not to send your photograph. I know you well,

and why should you spend money? Buy yourself rather something else. And now you write me that you receive few letters from me; but I write letters to you very often. And now I beg you, dear sister and brother-in-law, send my children to school, and let their eyes be rubbed.[1] . . .

HELENA BRYLSKA

1. As after sleep, so that they may see clearly. This is a very good expression of the peasant woman's attitude toward learning, when this is appreciative. Instruction is good because it makes [children] brighter in a general way, not because it makes [them] more fit for any practical purpose. It is perhaps the consequence of the fact that the appreciation of women is in general more subjective, bearing on the personality, rather than objective, bearing on work. At the same time the peasant man often shares the same attitude, which was, indeed, our own former attitude toward "academic culture," the "polished man," and the girls' "finishing school."

April 19 [1907?]

DEAR SISTER: . . . . You write, dear sister, that Józiek is ill with his eyes. It would be terribly painful for me if you should not send him, dear sister. And [their step]father would be terribly angry and terribly grieved, if they all may not come. He says, "I strive and strive and wish that they may come to us. Although I am not their own father I care for them as for my own [children], and God will not punish me as [he would do] if I did not wish to have anything to do with them." So I beg you very much, sister dear, send him, because I have heard and shall have to hear from my man, "Why should you not have them all with you? Later on any of them could say to himself that through his stepfather he became an orphan and does not see his mother."[1] So send him. If he is so terribly ill they will send him back from Iłłowo, but I do not think that they will send him back. They are on ship ticket and he goes to his mother, so I do not think that it will be so. Only send him, dear sister, and they will surely let him through. I beg you. Mr. Wiśniewski, very much, don't be anxious and afraid that you will have many difficulties. And at the frontier if you strike a bargain with a smuggler he can get ten persons through the frontier. And I will reward you for this. If he does not come it will be a terrible sorrow and trial for us, and a large expense, because they will not give us the money for this ship ticket back; and I shall ever bear a grief in my heart, that I endeavored to have this child and have it not. Remember, dear sister, send him to me, I beg you for the love [of God?]. And now you wrote that you will send me a shawl, but don't make any trouble about it for yourself and for the [man] who comes. May only all my children come; I don't wish anything more. As you grieve about your children, so I grieve about mine. And I beg you once more, send me all the children, because the ship tickets are sent for all of them in order that they may all come. We salute you all and we wish you every good. Both of us beg for all the children. We will reward you for it. Mr. Wiśniewski, if they ask you during the journey about anything, say only this, that you bring children to their parents. That is all; you don't need any other explanations. And now again, if God leads you happily through the water perhaps they will require somebody, mother or father, to come and meet you in New York; then they will ask, "Is it your father or mother?" Let them [the children] say, "It is our mother or father." And say Mr. Wiśniewski is my brother. Then all will be well, only don't give any other explanation than such as we request you to give. And now, dear sister, you write that perhaps they will send him back from Iłłowo. Well, then nothing can be done. It would be the will of God; he would be an orphan until his death and would never more see his mother. O my God, what a sorrow for me! But perhaps God will grant him to be let through. Prepare them all [for the journey], dear sister. I hope that he will get through. Your well-wishing and loving.

DĄBROWSKIS

[Helena Brylska's married name]

1. The stepfather's motive in having the children brought is not affection for the children, whom he does not know, and is something more than attachment to his wife. We have here, in fact, a good insight into the nature of the feeling of moral obligation in the peasant. It is, first, the religious fear of God, and second, the fear of a possible blame and reproach of the wronged persons. If there is the usual fear of public opinion, it is not expressed and certainly not very strong, since the man lives almost completely isolated from his community, while in normal peasant life this fear of public opinion is universally connected with the feeling of moral obligation. We have here a good proof that the crisis brought by emigration or any disintegration of communal life does not lead necessarily to a disintegration of morality. The explanation of the various results brought by the dissociation of the community (or family) in this respect is probably to be found in the fact that social appreciation is not the only sanction for the peasant, but is indissolubly connected, in various proportions, with self-appreciation, and in certain

conditions and for certain individuals this element of self-appreciation may develop strongly enough to substitute itself completely for the social appreciation. Thus, as we have seen in Adam Raczkowski, self-appreciation in the form of a feeling of personal importance, by substituting itself for familial solidarity, changes altruism from a duty into an expression of the personality. Here self-appreciation assumes the form of the feeling of righteousness before God and man. The source of the fear of the blame of the person wronged is not the same as that of the fear of social blame; in the first a magical background is still noticeable, while nothing like this can be detected in the second.

June 6 [1908?]

DEAR SISTER: I write as to a sister and I complain as to a sister about my children from the old country—those three boys. I did not have them with me, and I grieved continuously about them; and today again, on the other hand, my heart is bleeding. They will not listen to their mother. If they would listen, they would do well with me, But no, they wish only to run everywhere about the world, and I am ashamed before people that they are so bad. They arrived, I sent them to school, because it is obligatory to send them; if you don't do it the teacher comes and takes them by the collar. So they have been going, but the oldest was annoyed with the school: "No, mama, I will go to work." I say, "Go on to school." But "No!" and "No!" Without certificates from the school they won't let them work. I got certificates for the two oldest ones: "Go, if you wish." They worked for some time, but they got tired of work. One went with a Jew to ramble about corners [trading or amusing himself?], and for some days was not to be seen; I had to go and to search for him. The worst one of them is Stach; the two others are a little better. They were good in the beginning but now they know how to speak English, and their goodness is lost. I have no comfort at all. I complain [to you] as to a sister, perhaps you will relieve me at least with a letter, if you write me some words, dear sister.[1] We remain, well-wishing,

H. J. DĄBROWSKIS

1. In this letter we have the whole tragedy of the breakdown of old sentimental habits. There must have been a complex process of weakening relations between mother and children, due to the facts that in the mother there evidently coexist more or less independently the old sentimental habits and some new ones, acquired in America and in her second marriage, while in the children there is a rapid and more or less complete evolution from the old familial life to an individual independence. We . . . find elsewhere . . . the proof that the children were disappointed in their expectations when they came to their mother; there were

in her some new features which made her appear almost a stranger to them. On the other hand, the children lost their primitive attitudes even more rapidly and completely, and after some time the mother, from the standpoint of her old sentimental attitudes, began to see strangers in them. Probably this disintegration of the family was hastened by the lack of a father. At any rate, the result is that the mother feels the old set of her sentimental attitudes to a large extent objectless, and the disappointment with her children makes her cling more eagerly than ever to her sister—the only person of her whole family who is still a real link with her old life. This proves at the same time how much stronger the old sentimental habits are as compared with the new ones, and how much more difficult is the adaptation to new conditions for a woman than for a man. Compare her brother.

January 10 [1909, 1910, or 1911]

DEAR SISTER: . . . . I received the letter with the wafer and I thank you for thinking of me, dear sister. Now, dear sister and brother-in-law, don't be angry if I don't write to you very often, but I don't know how to write myself and before I ask somebody to write time passes away, but I try to answer you sometimes at least. You ask me how much my boys and my man earn. My man works in an iron foundry, he earns 9, 10, 12 roubles [dollars] sometimes, and the boys earn 4 or 5 roubles. My dear, in America it is no better than in our country: whoever does well, he does, and whoever does poorly, suffers misery everywhere. I do not suffer misery, thanks to God, but I do not have much pleasure either. Many people in our country think that in America everybody has much pleasure. No, it is just as in our country, and the churches are like ours, and in general everything is alike. We remain, well-wishing,

H. J. DĄBROWSKIS

My children, thanks to God, are not the worst now.[1]

1. The process of readaptation between mother and children begins, but it will never be complete: the mother cannot get rid of her old desire of authority and tendency to a complete unity of familial life, while the children, after their period of wildness, can neither come back to the traditional familial attitudes of the old country nor yet develop a new organization of their familial life in which individualism and solidarity would be harmoniously unified.

April 5 [1910 or 1911]

As to the children, two of them are very good children. One is working and gives his money [to me], the other is going to school, and learns well, but the third is not at home at all. Stach has been bad, is bad, and will be bad. So long as he was smaller, he remained more at home. I begged him, "Stach, remain at home with your mother." No, he runs away and loafs about. Well let him run. I had his eyes wiped [had him instructed] as well as I could; he can read, write, and speak English, quite like a gentleman. You say, "Beat." In America you are not allowed to beat; they can put you into a prison. Give them to eat, and don't beat—such is the law in America. Nothing can be done, and you advise to beat! Nothing can be done; if he is not good of himself, he is lost.

. . . I regret that I took the children from our country so soon. In our country perhaps they would have had some misery, and in America they have none, and because of this many become dissolute. In America children have a good life; they don't go to any pastures, but to school, and that is their whole work.[1] . . .

H. J. DĄBROWSKIS

1. Helena's statement is a good illustration of the changed conditions under which the parental authority is weakened. In Poland the children do light farm-work under the eye of their parents, while the American school is certainly a factor of emancipation.

August 7, 1911

. . . as to my children, I gave Maniek away to a school for 2 years. If he is good, I will take him [then], if he is not good, he will remain there till his twenty-first year. If he does his best and listens to what they tell him to do they will let him go sooner. If he does not listen, they will not let him go until his twenty-first year. I gave him away, dear sister, because he would not go to school and listen. I have always had trouble with him. I had to send him there, and perhaps he will become a [good] man. They teach reading and writing and different kinds of work. When he is older he will not suffer misery. I call on him frequently. He feels well. If he suffered misery there I would not allow this. The oldest is not with me, the second is not with me, I feared this one would run away from me, and I gave him away. He will the sooner learn to be reasonable, and he can become a man. . . .

H. J. DĄBROWSKIS

BORKOWSKI SERIES

The Borkowski case is a particularly interesting example of a situation in which the marriage group has almost ceased to be a part of the family and is no longer kept together by the familial organization, while the personal connection of husband and wife is not yet strong enough to make the group consistent.

The Borkowskis are city people. We do not know when the families of the husband and wife came to Warsaw—it may have been thirty years ago or three hundred—and their attitudes give us no cue to this problem. The fact is that we find here an almost complete lack of traditional elements, except religion. But this may be the result either of a loss of peasant traditions in the city or of a gradual disintegration of old city traditions under the influence of modern life. At any rate, Borkowski is a factory workman, not a guild member, so he has not even the vestiges of the traditions of the hand-worker class, which would be slight even if he were a member of a guild, as we see in the case of his friend, Stanisław R.

Although Borkowski and his wife have numerous relatives in the city or in the neighborhood, the members of neither family care much for one another. The lack of solidarity goes so far that Borkowski's brother has not written to him during a period of twenty years; otherwise the letters would have been preserved with the others. Compare this situation with the one which we find in the Markiewicz family. When Teofila, the wife, finds herself in an exceptionally bad situation, no one among her relatives helps her. They avoid even social relations with her, as a boresome, poor, ill-dressed, complaining old woman.

There is also nothing that could take the place of the community which we find in the country or in small towns. To be sure, everyone has a circle of acquaintances within which there is gossip—a poor imitation of social opinion—but there is nothing like the continuous relationship between the inhabitants of a village, and no periodic meetings. Social opinion has therefore little power, consistency, or vitality.

2:343–59, 36–67.

Clearly in these conditions marriage becomes a mere individual matter; its social side is limited to the religious sanction, to the few uncomplicated relations between the marriage group and the loose social environment, and to an exceptional intervention of this environment and of the state in the rare cases of criminal behavior. Within the large limits marked by these few social forms there is place enough for all the varieties which the relation between two individuals of different sex may assume. The nature of this relation will, of course, depend upon the personalities of the members and the sphere of their common interests. In the actual case, where the personalities of husband and wife are poor in traditions and poor in culture, their connection must be rather weak. When the first sensual attraction has disappeared, habit and the common interests of everyday life are the only links. But the emigration of the husband interrupted both of these, and a gradual dissolution of the conjugal bond became a psychological necessity.

We do not know the evolution through which the husband has passed, but we can easily guess it from the woman's letters. He evidently found a new sphere of interests in America; being a relatively intelligent, although not educated, man, he adapted himself successfully to the new conditions, and his life in Warsaw, where he did the same work but earned less and had less opportunity to express himself, must have appeared to him rather narrow—much more so, indeed, than in the case of a peasant, with the variety of work and the many concrete social interests which village life can give. Further, he seems to have felt rejuvenated in America, away from his wife, who was probably older than he. He dresses better, shaves his beard, and, as his wife expresses it, looks ten years younger. Probably, almost certainly, he has here a relation with another woman. Hence after a certain time there is nothing more left of the old affection toward his wife, and though for almost twenty years he writes from time to time and sends some money, he does it partly from pity, partly from a feeling of moral obligation. He does not make any great sacrifice; during the whole time he has sent her less than five hundred dollars, i.e., less than twenty-five dollars a year. But we must remember that he lacks any really strong motive to help her, for the feeling of obligation, not backed by the sanction of social opinion, cannot be strong in a man on this level of culture.

And he feels more and more that his wife is a useless burden to him—not only on account of money, but also as the only link with a past life which he evidently wants to forget, and perhaps also as a hindrance to marrying someone else. . . .

The letters give us a very good insight into the evolution of the woman. Without the backing of a family group she never feels that she has a right to claim her husband's fidelity, help, and protection. The higher moral view with regard to the conjugal relation is clearly not more strongly developed in her than in her husband and cannot be a substitute for the absent social norms. In the beginning she assumes implicitly that he will care for her after his emigration, since he cared for her at home. Later, when she realizes that things have changed, she appeals, not to his conjugal duty, but to his promise to help her and to his generosity. Still later, appeals to pity become her only resource, and when even this proves insufficient she uses additional arguments—promises of God's reward, threats of suicide, etc. Love is at no time appealed to. The nature of her claims changes also. First, she wants and expects her husband to come back rather than to take her to America; later she would be glad if he let her go to him, under someone's care (her affection is not strong enough to overcome her fear of the journey); still later, she ceases to expect to live with him and hopes only to see him once more; finally, it is enough for her to have from time to time his letters and money.

Another interesting point is her relation to her environment. As she has no social standing as a member of a family group, her social position is based exclusively on her marriage, i.e., upon the position of her husband, upon his attitude toward her, upon their having a home, etc. As soon as her husband leaves, her position is immediately lowered; she has no home and she does not represent much personally. But still he is expected to return or to take her to America, and thus her position is not yet so very low, because provisional. When, however, time passes and she remains alone, her social environment no longer takes her husband's possible return into account, and then her position depends exclusively upon his attitude toward her; every letter, photograph, or sum of money, which he sends influences her social standing positively, as proofs that he is still solidary with her, while every proof of his desire to get rid of her pushes her down in social opinion. Naturally, it would be quite different if she were able to fight for a position by herself, without being so exclusively dependent upon him. But, being a city woman, she is afraid of heavy work, not only because of its physical hardship, but also because she believes that it would lower her still more. On the other hand, she is unable to progress by skilled work and, moreover, apparently lacks energy. Being so completely dependent upon her husband, she wants him for herself alone; she seems to feel that every expression of his personality outside is a loss for her; she is hostile to all his friends and relatives.

All these features of the Borkowski marriage group are typical, resulting necessarily from the given social situation and the general characteristics of the personalities. Now, if they had children, the whole situation would be different. We shall find, indeed, in the next series [not included—ed.] analogous characters and an analogous social situation, and we shall see what an enormous importance the children have there—an incomparably greater one than in the traditional familial organization.

To Władysław Borkowski in America from His Wife in Poland

WARSAW, July 21, 1893

DEAR HUSBAND: I received your letter on July 4, which found me in usual health. Up to the present I live with the Rybickis. I am not very well satisfied, perhaps because I was accustomed to live for so many years quietly, with you alone.[1] And today you are at one end of the world and I at the other, so when I look at strange corners [surroundings], I don't know what to do from longing and regret. I comfort myself only that you won't forget me, that you will remain noble [generous] as you have been. You wanted me to go to the Borkowskis [his brother]. I was there. If they had only asked about you themselves! But nobody said a word, only I related.[2] . . . I have nothing more to write, only I beg you, my dear, write to me as often as you can about yourself, whether you are in good health and how you succeed, for this is my only pleasure; I have no other. I have only the sort of friends who think that I own thousands and from time to time someone comes to me, asking me to lend her a dozen roubles. . . . And everyone would borrow for eternity; I know them already. . . .

And now I bid you goodbye and wish you health and every good. Only don't forget me. Your sincerely well-wishing wife,

[TEOFILA BORKOWSKA]

1. Isolation has become habitual and desired. We do not find this in the peasant family. Of course, some privacy is always sought by the marriage group, but only for matters which, like the sexual relation, are more or less reserved by tradition as beyond the reach of other people's intrusion. And the amount of privacy claimed by the marriage group from the family is much smaller than that which it requires from the community. In short, privacy for the peasant is nothing but a certain socially sanctioned limitation of the social character of individual life. Here, on the contrary, it becomes a voluntary individual seclusion from the social life in general.

2. The disintegration of the family is certainly real, even if in the given case the writer puts a particular emphasis upon the indifference of her husband's relatives, in accordance with her tendency to keep him exclusively for herself.

April 12, 1894

DEAR HUSBAND: I received your letter on April 2, which found me in the best of health, and I wish you the same with my whole heart. Up to the present I thought and rejoiced that you would still come back to Warsaw, but since you write that you won't come, I comply with the will of God and with your will. I shall now count the days and weeks [until you take me to America]. May our Lord God grant it to happen as soon as possible, for I am truly worried. Such a sad life! I go almost to nobody, for as long as you were in Warsaw everything was different. Formerly we had friends, and everybody was glad to see us, while now, if I go to anybody, they are afraid I need something from them and they show me beforehand an indifferent face. . . . They all do it, even those who were so good formerly. Now they show themselves, as they are.[1] You write me to try to earn something with Władzia. But I have not earned yet a grosz from her. She says that people beg her to give them work for living alone, while I must pay 2 roubles for lodging, besides board.[2] So, my dear, I beg you, describe to me everything in detail, what I can take with me, what clothes, whether it is worth taking the fur, the [photographs in] frames, and other trifles. I will take the image and the cross, but I have heard that it was forbidden to take the chest. So please describe everything to me exactly. Your loving wife,

TEOFILA BORKOWSKA

1. As we have stated in the introduction, Teofila, not being a member of a family group, can have no other social recognition than that which results from her own or her husband's position. Her husband being away, the recognition which she had as his wife is reduced to almost nothing as is shown by the behavior of her environment and of which she complains. There are still two chances for her to keep at least some social standing. One is her husband's fidelity—sending of money, writing of letters, etc.—in a word, proofs that he remains solidary with her in spite of the separation and that the separation is only temporary, that he will either come back or take her to America. The second chance is to acquire a personal position by her own work.

2. Władzia is a cousin who has a millinery or dressmaking shop, in which Borkowski wants his wife to work as a seamstress.

August 8, 1895

DEAR HUSBAND: . . . . You won't believe how much I suffered when you did not write for some months. I thought that I should not live long enough to read your letter, but when I received the letter from you I wept with joy. But after reading it sadness overwhelmed me again. I thought that you had forgotten and would not write your address. But, thanks to God, it seems to me that my heavy sorrow and my terrible want are over. There is no work this year with Dobska at all, so I don't sew there at all. I earn sometimes a few złoty, but what does it mean when I must pay 3 roubles rent a month [in a room with three or four others]. In one place I had no money to pay for the lodging, and they took my bed. Now I sleep upon a borrowed bed. Moreover, they have levied hospital taxes in Warsaw, 1 rouble for a person yearly, so I must pay, for if you do not pay you must pay later 4 roubles of fine.

Before I received your letter, I went to the consul more than once, begging him to find you, what is going on with you. But he did not want to search for you until I paid him 5 roubles. But I did not have them and I had to remain in sadness. My dear, you ask for my photograph, but I can send it only when you send me a few roubles. But I beg you, send me yours as soon as possible. . . .

[TEOFILA]

October 2, 1895

DEAR HUSBAND: To the last letter which you wrote on July 13, I answered at once with great joy, for I thought that after so many months of my sorrow and crying and different other troubles the sun shone for me. But I see that it only joked, that I must suffer so up to my death. Up to the present I have never annoyed you [about money], for I knew that when you could, you would send me a few roubles. So I beg you, if you can, send me a few roubles as soon as possible, for I am in a situation without issue. . . . Your loving wife,

TEOFILA BORKOWSKA

January 28, 1896

DEAR HUSBAND: . . . . You reproach me for not answering you at once. My dear, I evidently did not do it through negligence, for you won't believe, I have not words enough to tell you, how much good you did me by sending that money, you saved me from some strange despair, because I waited for this money as for the salvation of my soul. Twelve roubles out of this money went for rent alone, for I must pay 3 roubles a month. Now they won't take less for a person, because apartments have gone up. And I have a corner where I must sit upon my bed. And in renting they say at once that I cannot cook, and ask me whether I will sit much at home. I have often such conditions for these 3 roubles that I cannot even boil a little water for my tea, but must remain the whole day living on dry food. . . .

TEOFILA BORKOWSKA

May 13 [1896]

DEAR HUSBAND: I received your letter . . . together with the photographs. You won't believe me what a joy and comfort it was for me when I saw you. It seemed to me in the first moment that I saw you alive. I received the money, i.e., 12 roubles, on April 1. I thank you for it heartily.

Now, dear Władek, as to my coming to you, if it were possible, I should be very glad, but imagine what a terrible difficulty it would be for me to start quite alone on such a far journey. You know that I am not very bold, nor very talkative either, so it would be very difficult for me to find my way alone.[1] For as to Rafalski, he won't go now; his plans are changed. He is offended with you for having written him about land instead of writing how much you earn and what work is there. He says: "Does he do any favor to me? He will send me a ship ticket when I send him 20 roubles. But if I wish I can buy a ticket myself." My dear, you ask me why I do not write you about Karol and his wife. I have nothing to write about them, for I know nothing. They don't come to me at all, they are afraid I might want something from them, so I don't go to them either. Since you left they have not invited me to any holidays or little parties which they arrange often. You know, Władek, I pray to God continually that He may inspire you with the wish to come back to Warsaw. After the crowning there will be amnesty, so you can come back, and you would certainly have work, for in the factory they are working on holidays and nights, and everybody says that it will last for some years still. So, my dear, perhaps you will change your mind and long for your native country. I heard that you promised it to Rafalski. I would wait patiently; I have suffered for 3 years, I would bear it for one more. . . . I have kept the box, the image of God's Mother, and the photographs as tokens. I did not sell your fur coat either; I keep it, for I think that you will perhaps walk in it about Warsaw. Although I was already in hard need, I did not sell it.[2] . . .

My dear, don't forget what I asked you for, because I need it very much and very soon. . . .

[TEOFILA]

1. Her helplessness, in contrast with the energy of country girls who undertake the journey to America even to marry unknown men, is perhaps partly constitutional.

2. The woman's desire to see her husband back in Warsaw rather than go to America is probably conditioned by other factors than her fear of traveling alone. She can imagine future happiness only in the same familiar conditions and environment in which she had lived happily before. Perhaps there is also some desire to get restitution for all the humiliations which she has to suffer, to have the same people who now neglect her to be the witnesses of her triumph.

July 10, 1896

DEAR WŁADEK: . . . . I don't know what it means that you don't answer the letter in which I thanked you for the photographs and the money which you sent me, 10, 11, and 12 roubles, the last before Easter. I sent you a letter on May 13, almost begging for a few roubles, for I spent these on medicines and the doctor, but not only did you not send me anything, you did not even answer, so I don't know what it means, whether you are offended with me for having asked you for these few roubles. But you have written yourself that you will send me [money] every month, and therefore I was more bold in asking you for it.[1] . . . Your always loving wife,

TEOFILA BORKOWSKA

1. She does not consider it her husband's duty to maintain her, as a peasant woman would do, but appeals merely to his promise.

December 2, 1896

DEAR HUSBAND: I inform you that I have already left the hospital and I am healthy enough, and I wish you the same. I received in the hospital the letter which you wrote on August 31. I rejoiced very much, for every letter from you is a day of joy for me, and I have no other joy now. Only I am very much pained that you reproach me for writing only about myself and nothing about any relatives or acquaintances. But what can I write about them, since they are all *państwo* [originally "lord and lady," then in general, "gentle people" or "rich people"] as compared with me, while I am quite alone, without husband, without home. When I left the hospital I did not know what to do with myself, without money and almost without roof, for I did not know what to do and what to pay for the lodging with.

My Władzio, don't be angry that I send registered letters, but you see you write so seldom I should think that my letter did not reach you and I could not learn, while so I am certain that you received it and I live at least with some hope that you will answer me. And now I am waiting for an answer to that letter which I wrote you when I was in the hospital, and I know that it reached you for it was registered. Evidently, dear Władek, you are so angry with me that you have not written for some months, while I sent you almost not a letter but a petition. So don't be angry with me, my dear husband, for to whom shall I appeal? And you made me bold yourself, for you promised me to send me a little, and I don't ask much, anything [a little] at least. And I beg your pardon once more, Władek, don't be angry with me, but answer me as soon as possible. As to the photograph, perhaps I shall earn a little, but only in the spring; then I would send you one, for now I have no money to go to the photograp[er].[1] . . .

[TEOFILA BORKOWSKA]

1. The absolute and painful dependence of the wife could hardly be better illustrated than by this letter.

May 19, 1897

DEAR HUSBAND: . . . . You write me that you are not sure whether I receive your money, because I don't write myself [with my own hand], only Mrs. Sliwińska [the woman from whom she rents] does. But you can be as sure as if I wrote with my own hand. She gives me every letter as soon as she receives it from the post, whether with money or not, and address them as always, because they are pure people. . . . I intentionally begged somebody else to write this letter in order that you might believe that I receive your letters and money. I beg you, dear Władek, write to me more often, for now you have not written for so long a time. My dear, write me whether you intend ever to come back to Warsaw? I often hear that some husband comes back to his family, and even whole families return. When I hear it my heart almost bursts open, because you don't write and won't return to your native country. Why, you are a Pole! . . . In Warsaw there is an enormous movement, all factories full of work, and for you also work is ready. Only come! . . . Your loving wife,

TEOFILA BORKOWSKA

September 26, 1897

DEAR HUSBAND: For God's sake, what does it mean that you don't answer? Kawecki called on me, for he also wrote to you and you gave him no answer, so he came to ask what you write to me, what is going on with you and how you succeed. He thought that you don't write to him because you have got very rich; he was curious, for he did not know how to judge you. Only when I told him that for half a year you have not written to me, he was also pained, fearing that something had happened to you. For I also grieved terribly [thinking] what had happened to you. For I don't think that you could have forgotten me totally, while I write you such supplications every time. So I repeat once more my begging. Answer me as soon as possible and send me anything you can.

So, my dear husband, don't be angry with me for writing to you so decidedly, but I have almost nobody except you. Although I have many relatives it is as if I had none, for you remember also what you got from your relatives when you were in need. Although you were only a child. . . . Your loving wife,

TEOFILA BORKOWSKA

May 24, 1898

DEAR WŁADEK: I received your letter on May 1, i.e., 15 roubles of money. They had searched for me for some weeks and could not find me, because you almost never address to Jan Sliwiński, but to Teofila Borkowska. I should not have received this money . . . only Sliwińska wondered why you had not written for almost a year. She found the postman and asked him whether he had never had a letter from America to Borkowska, and he said that he had one some weeks ago, but could not find [the person] and gave it back to the post office. There were two money orders, one of 15 roubles for Teofila Borkowska, and the other of 25 roubles for Teofila Bartowska [misaddressed]. They refused to give me the second, saying that it was not for me and kept it at the office. And as you sent no letter, I don't know myself whether these 25 roubles are for me or not. So I beg you, dear Władek, answer me the soonest possible whether you sent me these 25 roubles, and if you did, you must correct the name yourself. . . . Perhaps I suspect you, dear husband, and grieve that you have forgotten me, while it is perhaps unjust. Your always loving wife,

TEOFILA BORKOWSKA

Good by [in English; imitated from his letter].

September 12, 1898

DEAR HUSBAND: First I must thank you heartily for having helped me so much. I did not expect it at all, only I always thought that perhaps you had no money yourself and you could send me none. I only prayed to our Lord God to give you health and to bless you in all your intentions, for I knew that you would not desert me. And so it happened, for which I thank you heartily once more, and may our Lord God help you further in everything.

First I received the 15 roubles about which I wrote you. Then I received 25 roubles, when you corrected the name. And now I received 28 roubles through the Commercial Bank, for which I made some purchases, because for a long time I had bought nothing [no clothes, etc.] for myself. I am very happy through all this, but I should be still more happy if we could see each other some day and if it were in Warsaw.

You ask me what is the news in Warsaw. You would not recognize Warsaw—such movement and work, hundreds of big new houses. On Marszałkowska Street a score of very splendid houses, and a very beautiful church on Dzielna Street, and in the neighborhood of the Jesus Hospital they begin to build a church, and on Czerniakowska Street a church, and a politechnical school is opened in Warsaw, such as up to the present have been only abroad. Therefore there is movement and in factories everywhere much work. . . .

TEOFILA BORKOWSKA

May 12, 1899

DEAR HUSBAND: I received your letter . . . with 20 roubles and three photographs on April 4, for which I send you a hearty "God reward." I bear it always in my heart and thought and I always repeat it to everybody, that you were good and generous and you are so up to the present. I can be proud before everybody that you don't forget me[1] for which once more may our Lord God reward you. I beg only our Lord God that we may yet see each other once more. Write me, dear Władek, can I hope it? When I saw you in a cyclist dress in the photograph, I could hardly recognize you, you have got about 10 years younger, particularly because you had your beard shaved. But did you not regret your beard? . . . Your loving wife,

TEOFILA BORKOWSKA

1. We see how her social standing depends exclusively upon her husband's good will toward her. She does not succeed in getting position personally, hardly even tries, but clings desperately to the only thread which keeps her from falling definitely into the class of paupers and outcasts.

June 26, 1901

DEAR WŁADEK: I received the letter with 50 roubles, which you sent on January 25. Later, after many troubles and much walking, at the cost of 10 roubles, I got the pictures, for which I thank you heartily, first for the money, then for the picture. For you not only remember about my needs, but you caused me great pleasure. But for the picture only I thank you, for Karol [brother] and Lodzia [niece] are not satisfied at all, they would prefer a score or two of roubles.[1] Dear, Władek, I have not written for so long a time, for, to tell the truth, I don't dare to importune you so often. But you authorized me yourself, for you wrote me to write you whenever I needed money. So, dear Władek, I write you now. . . .

I don't live any longer with Karol and his wife, for it seemed to them that since I lived with them they ought to have a living out of me. But as I could not give them everything you sent me they began to behave toward me in an awful manner, so that at last they wanted to beat me. So I live now elsewhere. . . .

O, dear Władek, if it could happen some day, if you could come and take me with you! For myself I would not be able to go alone to you. And perhaps somebody from your side [of your family or friends] will go to America? Then I would willingly go with him to you. . . . Your loving wife,

TEOFILA BORKOWSKA

1. Again she tries, consciously or half-consciously, to weaken still more the connection between her husband and his family, in order to have him exclusively to herself. This method does not seem very wise, if we compare this situation with the peasant letters. Since the personal relation between husband and wife is not strong enough, the proper thing would be to strengthen as much as possible all the ties which attach him to his country.

April 23, 1904

DEAR HUSBAND: I received your letter with 60 roubles. . . . It rejoiced me on the one hand, but on the other hand grieved me very much. Believe me, dear Władek, that I had such a foreboding. When I divided the [Easter] egg with anybody, I wept, for I imagined always that you are so far away, alone, without family, and more than once you must feel very sad, as I do, and perhaps even sick, and there is nobody to care for you of your own people. And so it seemed to me continually, and suddenly Sliwińska brings me a letter. Really, my foreboding proved true. Believe me, dear Władek, that I even was not so glad to receive this money as grieved in learn-

ing that you are sick. You are often sick there, probably the climate
is bad for you. But I pray and beg our Lord God every day to give
you health and to make you still happy in your life. You are still
young, and up to the present you have not yet experienced any
good in your life. So may our Lord God give you every good, whatever you wish from Him, for your good heart.[1] God reward you for
the money which you sent me! Besides you, I had still another sorrow, for my brother Ignacy is dead. . . . I don't know even whether
you remember him. So people of my family begin to die. . . .

TEOFILA BORKOWSKA

1. This is apparently a resignation to the idea of a perpetual separation and
perhaps to the possibility of his being happy with another woman.

August 8, 1904

DEAR HUSBAND: For God's sake answer, what is going on with you.
This is the fourth letter which I send you, begging you for an answer, and you don't answer me even a word. I believe, dear husband,
that perhaps you are tired already with writing always and sending
money. But perhaps your Lord God will make you free soon. I wish
it myself, for I am also tired with worrying myself so in this world
and worrying you besides. Although you do not let me feel it, because you are good, yet I feel it myself, and whenever I receive
money from you I weep, for I am a burden to you and I can repay
you nothing except by praying God for your health and for happiness in your life.[1] . . . Your sincerely loving wife,

Good by   TEOFILA BORKOWSKA

1. Her conviction is more outspoken than in the preceding letter. A few words
from time to time and a little money to enable her to continue to live is all she
can claim.

November 25, 1906

DEAR HUSBAND: First, may God the Great reward you for your
good heart and your care for me, for truly it is nothing else but
the Divine Providence which through your person guards me. I
had not a whole rouble left, and moreover I got so sick that I was

taken unconscious to the hospital; nobody even among my acquaintances knew it. Only when I came back a little to health I
asked the nun to telephone to Sliwińska, and the latter when coming to me met the postman who gave her a letter and a money
order for 70 roubles. . . .

Perhaps you won't come here for ever, dear Władek, but at least
perhaps you will visit Warsaw and your friends, and so God will listen to me and I shall see you once more.[1] . . .

TEOFILA BORKOWSKA

1. Complete resignation, placing herself on the same basis as his friends.

March 1, 1907

DEAR HUSBAND: Again some months have passed and I have
no news from you. As long as you were in Chicago it seemed as if I
felt you nearer, but now [when you are in California] it seems to
me that you are so far that even by thought I cannot reach you. O,
my dear Władek, you cannot imagine how woeful it is to live so
alone, a woman left by everybody in the world. For if a woman is
poor she has no friends at all, even her family leaves her. I see nobody but Sliwińska from time to time, and nobody else ever comes
to me. Your loving wife,

TEOFILA BORKOWSKA

September 2, 1909

DEAR HUSBAND: For God's sake, what has happened? Since you
wrote last year and sent money in June . . . you sent money the second time in December , but no letter.

. . . . I beg you, dear husband, don't be angry, but I beg you, send
as soon as possible, what you can. Dear Władek, I know that you are
worth some thousands, for Mr. K. told me so. You could therefore
do to yourself and to me and to all your friends this pleasure, and
come at least on a visit to Warsaw. Now in Warsaw it is very quiet.

Good bye, dear husband, and may God give you everything the
best. Your loving wife,

TEOFILA BORKOWSKA

January 20, 1910

DEAR HUSBAND, MY BELOVED WŁADEK: I don't know why you do not want to write to me. Evidently you don't want to, for I have sent you 4 letters and begged and implored you to write a least a few words, but you don't write at all. Never yet, during so many years, has it been so. Now, toward the end of my life, for a year and 8 months you have not written a letter. Why, you could find a little time to write a few words! You sent money a year and two months ago and even then you did not write a word. Evidently you don't wish to care for me any more. And what can I do now, unhappy woman, since I cannot earn enough for my living. Here thousands of young people walk without work, and for me, in my advanced age, it is still more difficult. . . .

TEOFILA BORKOWSKA

August 6, 1910

DEAR HUSBAND: I write to you with great timidity, but despair obliges me to write so openly. I beg you, dear Władek, I beg you for God's sake, have pity and send me a little money, for I can find no way out. I tried to get from the Philanthropic Association at least a few tickets for a few pounds of bread and a few pints of gruel monthly, but they refused me, for they learned that I have a husband. They say that it is for them all the same whether this husband is in Warsaw or in America, but I have a husband. So I don't know what to do with myself. I have no work, for now even a poor servant maid wants [her dresses] to be sewn on a machine with different adornments, for such is the fashion. And, to tell the truth, I begin to lose my eyes with sewing and crying. . . .

TEOFILA BORKOWSKA

Dear husband, write me whether you will come some day to Warsaw? It is true that you have put aside some money, but on the other hand you are far away from your family and from your land. Write me, dear Władek; let me at least have some illusion that I shall still see you.

October 13, 1910

DEAR HUSBAND: A few weeks ago I sent you a letter, or rather a supplication, asking you to have pity and to send me some money. But you, Władek, did not answer me a word. I don't know what to think. I think that you are tired perhaps with having cared for me for so long a time. But have pity and send me something and don't forget me. Perhaps soon things will come to an end with me and I shall go aside from your way. Write me, dear Władek, what is the news with you. Perhaps you are sick and therefore don't answer. Answer, my beloved, my dear benefactor, and send me some money. . . .

TEOFILA BORKOWSKA

April 20, 1911

DEAR HUSBAND: I wrote you four letters and in every one I implored you to write me at least a few words, and I cannot prevail upon you. So, my dear husband, have pity on me, I implore you, and send me a little money, for strange things come already to my head, and I tell you openly that it is from hunger. For a long time I have not had a penny of my own, only a few roubles of debt which I borrow, a few złoty at once. But as it seems to other people that you won't send me any more, so I don't dare to borrow, and they make excuses and don't want to lend me. So I beg you, send as soon as possible, or else I will probably take my life away. On Easter I should not have had a bit of dry bread if Sliwińska had not give me, and she also has nothing, lives only by the mercy of her children.[1] . . .

TEOFILA BORKOWSKA

1. The next letter, here omitted, shows that he sent her some money—ed.

July 12, 1912

DEAR HUSBAND: Have pity upon me, for I am already barefooted and naked. They have taken everything for the rent, even the pillow from under my head; only a small pillow is left. Have pity, dear Władek, and send me some money! You won't let me die from hunger, for I know that you have a merciful and noble heart, only perhaps somebody incites you. Why, I have not much longer to live, for with such a hunger as I suffer now I shall not hold out long. So I implore you, dear husband, have pity and listen to my imploring, for you are the second after God, to whom I pray every day.

Good by, dear husband. Be happy. Your loving wife,

TEOFILA BORKOWSKA

PART
3

SOCIAL DISORGANIZATION
IN THE UNITED STATES

This section presents two case records from Chicago charity organizations: one for economic dependency, or welfare, and one for marital breakup. Although the documents are valuable in their own right, in each case they are followed by extremely interesting analyses that stress the weakness of the community in America in comparison to its strength in Poland. In the later part of the twentieth century, there was considerable concern that government action weakened family life. Thomas and Znaniecki superficially shared this view—insofar as community ties remained strong.

MEYER FAMILY

Mr. Meyer, a German Pole, born of peasant parents, came to this country at the age of 23 years [in 1886]. His older brother who had preceded him several years had settled on a farm in the outskirts of Chicago and by dint of hard labor and strict economy now owns 80 acres of good land and is making a comfortable living. Needless to say he is a respectable citizen. This brother sent the necessary funds to our Mr. Meyer in order that he, too, might have a chance. Up to date this money has not been returned.

On arriving, Mr. Meyer was offered a chance to live with his brother but the lure of a large city seemed too great and Mr. Meyer, although unskilled in any line, took up common laboring work in Chicago, living in a more or less congested neighborhood. We know nothing, unfortunately, of his employment record until ten years later when he married a young German Polish woman, 25 years old. Mrs. Meyer, an illiterate woman, had been in America six years at the time of her marriage. She had for two years prior to her marriage done housework. . . .

The first application for assistance occurred in 1898 [2 years after the marriage] when Mrs. Meyer came to the Relief and Aid Society of Chicago asking rent. Mr. Meyer had been out of work for 3 months. There was one child [Mary], 13 months old.

Nothing seems to have been done at this time. Other children were born, Tillie in 1899, Theodore in 1903, Bruno in 1908, and Eddie in 1911.

January 30, 1908, Mrs. Meyer came to the office of the United Charities. Husband had not worked for 4 years, mentally slightly abnormal. She had recently begged but had usually worked very hard. Mary picking coal from tracks. . . . [Helped by United Charities and County Agent.]

January 3, 1909, visited. Man at home, says he had to care for children while wife went out to work. Told him he must get work at once as the doctor says he is able to work. [He had a severe fall

___
5:190–98, 205–9.

several years ago which left him partly paralyzed, but the doctor reports that the man's greatest trouble is laziness.] . . .

November 1, 1910, Miss Campbell, whose mother has employed Mrs. Meyer for years, in office to ask me if man cannot be sent to Bridewell [House of Correction]; says woman has come to work with arms black and blue from beatings. . . . Mrs. Meyer says man has not worked for more than 2 months at a time in the 19 years of his married life; says he taunts her with the fact that she must work while he stays at home.

November 3, 1910 . . . man given 60 days in Bridewell.

January 13, 1911, visitor heard . . . that the man had taken carbolic acid New Year's Eve. Asked woman about this. At first she did not want to tell but finally acknowledged it; says he took 20c. worth of poison while she was at work. Children yelled when he fell and the landlord came in. . . . He got better and returned home again. Woman says man sleeps during the day and will not sleep at night, annoying her considerably, thus causing her to lose considerable sleep. Quarrels with her and uses vile language in the presence of the children.

January 16, 1911, man in office asking to be arrested; said he is unable to live with woman any longer. [Jealous of unmarried man who calls on woman.] . . . [Man complained woman took some clothes from office of the United Charities, where she was employed as janitress.] Woman acknowledged doing this and said man told her to take anything she could lay her hands on as she did not receive enough salary for the amount of work she did. . . . While woman was away at work man burned all the bedding, lace curtains, new veil daughter had received at Xmas, insurance policies, all the woman's clothes he could get ahold of, and some of the children's clothes; also broke a clock and bit up woman's wedding ring. . . .

March 7, 1911, man given year in Bridewell. [The visitor received the following letter from him dated March 28, 1911.] Dear Friend: . . . I am thankful that you put me here. I learned how to work. Please see my wife and tell her that I will take care of my children and her if she will please get me out. I don't care much about myself but I always worry about my children and her. I did not know how to appreciate when I could see my wife and children every day. If she gets me out this time I will know how to take care of her. I don't want my children to be left orphans while they are young. [A letter dated May 5, 1911 says] I think a year too much for a man of may age. And not being my fault at all. So I thought of asking you for a favor and try and cut it to six months . . . seeing this my first time ever arrested and being in Chicago 20 years. I think I am in teal [entitled] to a chance. . . . [Another letter under date of December 23 is as follows:] Would you be so kind as to tell my wife that I am sick in the hospital hear and send her out hear to see me and give me a visset and have her bring my little Boy Bruno. I want to see him very bad. I haven't seen him in so long. . . . You will half to excuse me for sending the letter to you and putting you to so much trubble but I have ben hear so long I have forgot the number where I live. . . .

January 31, 1912, man in office, came directly from the Bridewell without visiting his home. . . . Told him that his wife did not wish him in the home and that he would have to get a position and stay at work for a month or two and give money into the home before United Charities would give consent to his return. [He stayed a few days at the Christian Industrial League, then refused to stay there any longer and went to his sister.]

February 5, 1912, visited sister . . . not willing to keep man there. Said he had a wife and children and ought to be at home with them. Man said he would take steps through court to get Bruno, that he was nearly insane to think he could not see them when he was released from the Bridewell. . . .

February 8, 1912, woman in office; said man had come home the day before at noon . . . and the children let him in. When she came home he knelt before her and kissed her hands and begged her to allow him to remain. Because he humbled himself to kneel before her she weakened and told him if he worked he could stay.

February 9, 1912, man in office asking clothing; said he secured work at $1.50 a day. Says he had no shoes and has to work outside in the wet and also that his feet hurt him. [He quit in a week and did not seem to make much effort to find work in spite of threats of the United Charities to have him arrested if he did not.]

March 14, 1912, Mary in office first thing in the morning to say that her father tore good overcoat into strips last night and burned it in the stove; that early this morning when they were all asleep in the house, he tore the curtains down and cut them, cut some of woman's clothing into strips, poured kerosene over feather beds, slashed the leather seats of the four dining room chairs and did other damage of this sort. [Threatened to buy pistol and kill Mrs. Meyer.] . . . Mrs. Meyer frightened and nervous and broken-hearted over the loss. . . . [Later Mary phones that her father has come home and is sitting quietly in the kitchen.] Visited. Mr. Meyer announced that he had nothing to say for himself except that 'the woman got the best of it and had everything her way.' He stated that he knew the patrol was coming for him that day and wished to 'fix' things for his wife, that he 'had not done much but had done something.' His attitude in the matter was one of spite and the attitude of his wife toward him unusually fine. Despite all that had happened she was rather gentle and almost pathetic in her statement of the case. . . .

March 15, 1912, case tried in court. Man had no excuse to give and did not attempt to defend himself before Judge other than to make the statement that 'there was a God in Heaven.' Was given $100 and costs; sent to House of Correction. . . .

December 12, 1912, a neighbor phones saying Mr. Meyer home and as Mrs. Meyer wanted to put him out again he beat her unmercifully [with a poker].

December 24, 1912, woman says man was arrested. . . . Statement by Joseph Meyer to the trial judge: "Yesterday, the 19th of January, was the twenty-second anniversary of my wedding to my wife, Martha, from whom I became an outcast through the entrance of a former old country schoolmate and friend who arrived here two years ago from German Poland, and who has won my wife's affections. And between my wife and this man they have connived to have me sent to the Bridewell upon mere allegation without foundation or truth. I was never given an interpreter and it seems that the statements of my wife were sufficient evidence to have me sentenced to serve first 2 months, the second time one year, and the third time 6 months. . . . My wife has often said that she works for rich people and can through their influence dispose of me as she sees fit, as it only takes her five minutes to make a complaint and they will attend to the rest. For over 2 years my wife refused absolutely to do her family duty by me and upon my return from the Bridewell the second time my wife had another child, a boy by this said friend, and cooly explained it was none of my business. In her attentions to this man she neglects my children and demoralizes their moral standard. I am now well and able to work and willing to work for the good of the children that God has bestowed upon me, but my wife is again attempting to have me sentenced in order to have me out of the way so she can pursue the course of her new devotion. As I said before, through the lack of having had an opportunity to explain myself from court through an interpreter, I have been exiled from my family and existed a convict for the time stated. My record in the Bridewell is, of course, procurable and shows that I received 54 days' credit for exemplary conduct. I have never been a drinking man. I am not having this letter written for me because I bear malice to the courts but I must seek some way of obtaining justice." [The Criminal Court Judge, upon the receipt of a certificate from the County Jail physician that Mr. Meyer was insane, turned the case over the the Detention Court. Mr. Meyer wrote the Legal Aid Society asking for an attorney to defend him.] They had felt after a conversation with him that he was not right mentally and asked Mental Hygiene to have an examination made. . . .

February 14, 1913, visited Detention Court. Man was sent to Kankakee [insane asylum]. After sentence was pronounced woman and Mary were hysterical; said they had never wanted him to go and they would not leave the court unless he was released. Woman's cousin told Mr. Moore that Mary is not working . . . and that she is making her mother's life miserable [she had started to work when 14 years old but was dismissed from position with Mary Crane Nursery because she was untruthful and stole several small articles and some money. The United Charities, in their resume of the situation for the court said] Mary . . . begins to show something of her father's temperament. . . . The child's confidence has never been gained. She has always taken her father's side and her mother is worried over her as she feels she is untrustworthy, is rouging her cheeks, and not coming home directly from her work. She is a woman whose enjoyment of household possessions is undiminished by the miseries of her domestic experience, as is a natural coquetry which she has always possessed. We believe that this is an innocent attribute and that all her husband's accusations of infidelity are the suspicions inevitably resulting from sexual obsession in a man otherwise unoccupied for 20 years. He has, undoubtedly, a diseased mind.

April 3, 1913, woman says that Mary did not go to work today as the paint made her sick. Asked that we call up the firm and verify this. Mary had been to Miss Farrell to get suit which had been promised her, but failed to see Miss Farrell and insisted upon getting a coat for which she agreed to pay $8 on the installment plan. An agent came to the house to collect for this and Mary behaved so badly, screaming and crying that woman finally paid him $2. Mary now has the suit from Miss Farrell and woman wishes to return the coat but she refuses to do so. [Mary discharged from present position because it was proved she stole from one of the girls. Mary refused to take housework offered her.]

June 9, 1913, woman in office in great distress; says Mary has not worked at all at the hat factory [as she had pretended]. . . . Has been going with a girl who worked there. The girls say the employer is an evil man and showed them a check book and said they could draw what they liked. . . . Mary [refused to let him kiss her but] stole this check book and on the 29th forged a check for $12 which she brought her mother saying it was her pay. On the 2nd she forged another check for $11; $6 of this she gave to her mother and $5 she spent at Riverview Park. . . .

July 29, 1913. . . . Probation Officer says Mary lost her job on the 25th, that one of the girls had loaned Mary a ring and when the time came for Mary to restore it, Mary could not find it. . . . [A report from Kankakee that Meyer had escaped was followed by a letter saying] 'he escaped one evening but returned of his own free will at bedtime and has since been residing in the Institution.' . . .

January 17, 1914, Mary brought home $6 on the 14th but insisted upon $4 being returned to her and with this she bought a very elaborate hat of black velvet and gold lace. Talked with Mary. She was very defiant and said that she would spend her money on clothing until she had something to wear. Was not satisfied with the coat that United Charities had given her from secondhand store. Said she would keep her money until she could buy a new style coat. Told her that if she did so the United Charities would not help with food.

January 22, 1914, Mrs. Meyer in tears. The forelady at the shop where Mary works telephoned that Mary had gotten married in court today. . . . Mary gave the date of her birth as December 18, 1895 [instead of 1896] and signed the affidavit herself. . . .

January 30, 1914, visited. Asked Mrs. Meyer to take a position. . . . Suggested Mary could stay and take care of the children. . . . Mary was at first very unwilling to consent to the plan. While the visitor was there Mr. Andersen [her husband] came in. He agreed to the plan at least temporarily.

February 4, 1914, Mrs. Meyer in office. Says the work is too hard at the present situation and she is not earning enough to feed the children. Mary has had to give her money and she is ashamed and sorry. She feels too nervous to work and wants United Charities to get Mr. Meyer out of asylum to support her. Jennie, her niece, took her to visit him and she found him nicely dressed and sober, doing teaming work. He promised never to drink and to support the family.

A letter written by the United Charities June 16, 1914, states: "We have found her this spring in a peculiar mental condition due, we think, to sheer discouragement and a feeling of having been defeated in life. All of her home furnishings are dilapidated and of long usage, because of her inability to replace them. She has been a woman who always took a peculiar delight in her home and longed to have it furnished daintily so that it did not compare so poorly with the homes where she has worked. We feel now that if we might help her replenish her linen and some of her household supplies we might be able to tide over their period of discouragement and help her to feel that life was again worth living." . . .

August 19, 1914, Mrs. Meyer and Mary in office. [Mary very well dressed and living in her own apartment.] Mary says she has been helping her mother continually with food and clothing. Her husband makes $19 a week but she has to pay $17 rent and $5 a week on her furniture. She also has to save money because she is now several months pregnant. Her husband wishes her to have a doctor. She is planning to have a midwife because it is cheaper. Advised her not to do this. . . . During a period of unemployment for her husband she refused to seek aid at her mother's suggestion as she felt too proud. . . .

November 13, 1915. Tillie still earns $4 a week. . . . Must buy new dress [refuses to wear dresses given by charity as being old fashioned—same as Mary]. For lack of satisfactory dress she has not gone to church for 3 weeks. Mrs. Meyer fears she will slip away from church unless allowed clothes she wants. Her [Mrs. Meyer's] ideas become more and more erratic. She said she wishes she were dead, had only trouble.

For the past year the church [Irish, not Polish, for the latter always demanded money instead of giving assistance] has had a decided influence over Mrs. Meyer. Her children attend the parochial school and the priest has taken a very active interest in their welfare. . . . The family lives in a less congested district and although Mrs. Meyer is still very nervous and frequently complains the whole complexion of the family has changed. She is very interested in a mother's cooking class started last winter. . . and is also being taught to write by her 12 year old son. . . . If the man remains in Kankakee and the children keep well, we feel sure the family will eventually become self-supporting. It is surely the highest point as far as the standard of living is concerned. . . . The present system of County relief cannot but have a debasing effect upon the family, particularly upon the children who frequently must accompany the mother in order to bring home the dole of inadequate rations. . . . Mary is a good housewife and a sensible mother. She is contented and happy and her ideals are considerably higher, due directly to her husband.

From the *Records of the United Charities of Chicago.*

[Cases such as this one would not] lead to abnormal behavior in the usual conditions of peasant life in Poland. However disabled physically an individual may be . . . there is some place for him in the family economy of peasant life, even if it is only the supervision of children in the absence of parents. His position may be inferior but not abnormal in consequence of the mere fact that his work is not equivalent to the expense of his support, and even if he cannot work at all he is dependent only on the family of which he is a rightful member, and his dependence is a simple and common social fact, implying no feeling of sacrifice on the part of those who support him and little feeling of humiliation on his own part. There is, on the other hand, no tendency to exaggerate one's own disability in order to escape work, since the individual is interested in the results of his work as benefiting his own group and is willing to do as much as he can.

Here the social situation is radically different. American society has no place for the disabled except the hospital. But the hospital has traditionally meant pauperization in the peasant consciousness, and he refuses to go as long as he has some self-respect preserved.

When American agencies compel him to go, he feels himself pushed down below the level of economic normality. As a reaction he may cease to care for any standards and be ready to beg or steal in order to escape that ultimate humiliation. Even a temporary disability, by reinforcing the general impression of insecurity brought by American conditions, produces an attitude of despondency which may even lead to suicide. We know cases in which suicide could not be ascribed to any other causes.

The Polish-American society counteracts this cause of economic demoralization in a considerable measure by its mutual health insurance system without which a very large proportion of cases of temporary disability would be followed by economic decadence. But where the sickness benefit does not exist or is economically insufficient, and particularly in cases where the disability though only partial is permanent, society offers no preventive mechanism of any kind. Even if the individual or marriage group has relatives in this country, the large family has no longer its old significance in matters of social solidarity and the attempts of American institutions to compel relatives to help the disabled are entirely hopeless. The reasons are clear. In the old country economic life was included in and subordinated to social relations, and economic solidarity was one of the necessary manifestations of a deeper unity of the large family which implied common responsibility and prestige, reciprocal response, community of traditions, similarity of occupations, etc.—a complex and indivisible set of attitudes. Here economic interests become dissolved from other interests and individualized; common prestige is no longer required, for the large family is not enough of a unit in the eyes of the community in which its members are scattered. Each member follows his own course of action, has a different set of interests, and whatever feeling of social cohesion is left is not sufficient to induce the individuals or marriage groups to support the disabled relatives against their own private economic interests.

In cases of mental abnormality or subnormality the role of social conditions and of the individual's own attitudes is even more clearly manifested than in those of physical disability. [Mental incapacity in a peasant woman, for example,] would not have led her into any trouble in the stable and regulated conditions of traditional peasant life in Poland. It would not have prevented her from acquiring the minimum of habits necessary in her position in the family and this position itself could have been adapted with the help of the large family to her abilities, however low. It is the novelty of the situations which she has to face in this country that makes her mental incapacity a factor of economic demoralization. Meyer was, of course, more or less abnormal temperamentally, which probably would have interfered to a considerable degree with his economic success and the harmony of his family life if he had lived in Poland. But he certainly would have remained a sufficiently steady and controllable member of his group to make any extraordinary measures against him unnecessary, whereas here his abnormality not only becomes an almost insuperable handicap by preventing him from constructing without social help a new permanent economic life organization adapted to the new conditions, but everything that happens to him out of the traditional order to which he has been accustomed increases his inability to define the situations which surge up in the course of his life, breaks whatever remnants of normal habits he had left, and drives him finally into a mental chaos and emotional despair actually verging on insanity. No wonder that at last the prison and the insane asylum are welcomed as bringing rest and relief in the form of a simple and regular life organization with no longer new and incomprehensible problems to solve at every step.

MICHALSKI FAMILY

Minnie and Stanley Michalski were very young when they were married. Shortly after their marriage a friend of Stanley's, a young man named Frank Kornacki, came to see them. He called about a half dozen times. One Monday in January, 1912, he came to the house at noon time. Young Mrs. Michalski was at home alone doing the washing. Whether or not he forced her to have sexual relations with him it is hard to say. She later claimed that she resisted him, but that he held her mouth with one hand so firmly she could

5:232–35, 265–70.

not scream and as she was 5 months pregnant she did not dare struggle to prevent him. She did not tell her husband of this. The child was born and named Helen.

One Sunday in August of the same year, Kornacki and Michalski were gambling together in a saloon. Michalski had won $8 when Kornacki, half drunk, offered to tell him "something" for the return of the $8. He then told of his intercourse with Mrs. Michalski. Michalski went home almost crazy and choked his wife until she told him the truth. His fury know no bounds. He would not believe that she had been without fault in the affair and ordered her to have Kornacki arrested for rape, refusing to live with her unless his former friend was punished. The warrant, however, was refused. He was especially enraged because the attack had happened during her pregnancy, and as she was at this time again pregnant she had an abortion performed to pacify him. He thereupon allowed her to return and they lived together for 2 years more. Then he left her, promising her $5 a week for the support of the child.

Mrs. Michalski appealed to the Legal Aid Society to assist her to get more money from her husband. Michalski answered in person the society's letter and made a very good impression on the interviewer, a new and inexperienced girl who was "very sorry for him." He insisted he loved his wife dearly but could not live with her. She had admitted to him having relations twice with some man and he simply could not forget that. Besides, every time he went out with her he imagined she was flirting and making some engagements with men. He concluded by offering to bring his wife to the office of the society "to talk the matter over." This he did. He refused more money and urged Mrs. Michalski to get a divorce, nobly promising to produce conclusive evidence of his unfaithfulness to her.

Nevertheless, the Michalski family tried living together once more, rented a flat, and bought new furniture. After 2 weeks Stanley Michalski left and his wife went to the Legal Aid Society to complain that he was running around with another woman and giving her only $5 a week. She was now willing to get a divorce. Nothing was done in the matter, however. Six months later she again applied to the society. The night before her husband had come to her flat and threatened to kill her and Helen. He turned on the gas and tried to choke her into unconsciousness, but she screamed so loudly that he became alarmed and left, seizing a photograph of himself that was hanging on the wall and taking the child with him. Mrs. Michalski called a policeman, arrested him, and got the child back.

Shortly after this, Michalski, who had become manager for the company he was working with, gave his wife a job in his office at $7.00 a week—this to avoid paying anything toward the support of the child. She soon lost her work, and he did not resume payments. The Legal Aid Society sent for him. He said he was unable to work, that he had contracted syphilis from some woman he lived with, was undergoing treatments for it, and would probably have to have an operation. He insisted that his wife was living immorally and told of catching a man partly undressed in her closet once when he called at her flat with a policeman. He wanted to arrest the man but was afraid of involving his wife. Some months later, Michalski went to the office of the Legal Aid Society and demanded the record of the case. He wished to see whether the record contained any admissions by his wife of her immorality, meaning to use such admissions as the basis for a divorce. When this request was naturally refused, he became very much excited and charged the society with always "shielding the woman."

Another 6 months went by. The divorce had been granted without a contest. Much testimony had been produced as to Michalski's good character and Mrs. Michalski's immoral conduct. Michalski's brother and a young girl had testified that one evening they had all been drinking and were playing hide and seek when Mrs. Michalski invited an 18-year-old boy into her bedroom and had intercourse with him. At first Mrs. Michalski denied this and offered to bring the boy in question to court to refute the story, but when more closely questioned by the Legal Aid attorney and shown the dangers of perjury she admitted it was true. But she implored the society to get the order of court giving the custody of the child to its father set aside. She said, with tears in her eyes, that the child meant everything in the world to her. When, a few days later, Michalski took the child from her, her despair was so real and so pitiful that the society determined to contest the divorce for her. The decree already entered was set aside on a preliminary showing of Michalski's bad habits. In preparation for the final hearing the Legal Aid attorney called on the girl for whom Michalski had left his wife. She did not resent the suggestion that she come to court to tell of her relations with Michalski. She "felt sorry for poor Minnie and would be glad to help her out," but it was a most inauspicious moment, as she was suing her own husband for a divorce and she did not wish to be placed in the situation of telling the same judge in Minnie's case that she was an immoral woman and in her own case that she was an irreproachable wife seeking separation from an undeserving husband. She finally agreed that if her own divorce "went through all right," she would consider helping "Minnie." But on no account was she to be subpoenaed, for if she was forced to testify against her wishes she would tell so much that neither Minnie nor her husband would be allowed to keep the child. A few weeks later Mrs. Michalski said Stella refused to help her, for Stanley had promised to marry her if she should get another decree of divorce. This was not the only promise of marriage that Stanley made pending his divorce.

Mrs. Michalski was allowed by the court order to see the child and once she kidnapped it. The Legal Aid Society obtained a court order allowing her to keep it. Neither Michalski nor his attorney appeared in court to contest the matter.

From the *Records of the Chicago Legal Aid Society.*

An entirely new element is introduced into the conjugal life of the Polish immigrant by the interference of the state, which from his standpoint includes not only court and police action but also the activities of private or half-private American institutions, because he can seldom distinguish a purely social institution from one maintained by the state, particularly as the former does or can, or at least is thought to be able to make use of courts and police. None of the other factors of conjugal disorganization has an equally uniform and general destructive effect upon marriage. After a careful study of many hundreds of cases, we have not found a single instance where official interference strengthened the conjugal bond. If occasionally some improvement seems to follow institutional action, it does not come because of, but in spite of this action. Sometimes it is due to some constructive economic or social influences, sometimes again the situation at the moment when brought to public attention was not really as bad as it seemed and a spontaneous readjustment was possible. In a great majority of cases, however, no detailed analysis is needed to notice the immediate additional strain which actual or threatened state interference puts upon the marriage bond.

The explanation of this is easy. The social control to which a marriage group in the old country is subjected by the families and the community bears upon this group as a unit and has the interests of this unit in view. The role of the social milieu is not to step between husband and wife and arbitrate between their personal claims as those of separate individuals, but to uphold their union when threatened by the action of either. The misbehaving individual is made to feel that he sins against the sacredness of marriage, not that he is wrong in his contest with another individual. Therefore the control of the old social milieu increases the institutional significance of the conjugal bond. On the contrary, the interference of the American institution means an arbitration between husband and wife, who are treated, officially and unofficially, as contesting parties, as individuals between whose claims a just balance should be established. This, for the consciousness of the immigrant, puts the whole matter at once not upon the basis of solidarity but upon that of a fight where each party wants to get the best of its opponent by whatever means possible. This impression is strengthened by what seems to be the official and foreign character of the interfering institutions, making any appeals to solidarity meaningless, because the social worker or the judge himself is not a member of the community and has no direct, vital interest in the marriage group. Moreover, the action of American institutions differs in nature from that of a Polish community by being sporadic and putting the matter on a rational basis, whereas the old social milieu acted continuously and by emotional suggestions rather than by reasoning.

Thus, direct or indirect state interference unavoidably *undermines* the institutional significance and traditional social sacredness of marriage. It does it even in the rare cases when it is well informed. But usually the conditions are aggravated by the ignorance of Polish peasant traditions and mores which characterizes the best intentioned and idealistic social workers and court officials. It is still worse, of course, in those happily rare cases where the representatives of American institutions lack tact and human interest. And any mistake or injustice committed by those in authority is apt to be exaggerated and misunderstood by the individual himself and becomes further, often most absurdly, misinterpreted by the social opinion of the immigrant community.

This is not all. Certain predominant tendencies manifested by

American institutions when interfering with conjugal life have already given birth among Polish immigrants to new social attitudes which constitute a predisposition most favorable to further conjugal troubles. Besides the idea of the instability of American marriage—a result of civil marriage and divorce—the most important of these are the exaggerated feeling of coercive power on the part of the woman and the corresponding feeling in the man that conjugal obligations are a matter of legal coercion but not of moral duty.

The consciousness that she can have her husband arrested any time she wishes on charges of nonsupport, disorderly conduct, or adultery is for the woman an entirely new experience. Though under the old system she had in fact a part in the management of common affairs almost equal to that of the man, yet in cases of explicit disagreement the man had the formal right of coercing her, whereas she could only work by suggestion and persuasion, or appeal to the large family. Now not only can she refuse to be coerced, since the only actual instruments of coercion which the man has left after the disorganizations of the large family—use of physical strength and withholding the means of subsistence—are prohibited by law, but she can actually coerce the man into doing what she wants by using any act of violence, drunkenness, or economic negligence of his as a pretext for a warrant. No wonder that she is tempted to use her newly acquired power whenever she quarrels with her husband, and her women friends and acquaintances, moved by sex solidarity, frequently stimulate her to take legal action. Such action is, of course, radically contrary to the traditional significance of marriage, but this significance is weak and apt to be forgotten at a moment of wrath, since there is no large family to keep it always alive. And the action once taken is irreparable, for the husband will never forget or entirely forgive an act which introduced foreign official interference into the privacy of his conjugal relations, humiliated his feeling of masculine dignity, and put him for the time of his arrest on the same basis as a criminal. If the arrest is made by a girl on a bastardy charge, the offence seems less grievous since there is no break of family solidarity; the girl does not owe obedience, and in most such cases the whole relation was already on a fighting basis before the arrest. A marriage performed in court under such conditions is, of course, usually a failure—as our materials show—but if the girl does not prove too contentious or insistent upon her rights, the relation may be established later, voluntarily and without legal pressure, whereas a conjugal bond is virtually broken by the husband's arrest. The man may be cowed into submission by fear, but his marriage relation has ceased to imply any familial solidarity in his eyes and is no longer a voluntary union but an enforced cohabitation and economic contribution which taken together appear much akin to serfdom. Naturally, unless much attached to his children or indolent by temperament, he tends to run away at the first opportunity. And the popularization of such facts and attitudes among the immigrants has resulted in the tendency of men to waive all idea of permanent duty connected with marriage. There is no use in trying to make an immigrant accept in this respect the formal idea of contract and admit the principle that by marrying he has undertaken certain lifelong obligations, for obligation is significant for him only as long as it is a part of the organization of the primary social group to which he belongs. American law treats him and his wife as isolated individuals, not as primary group members and between isolated individuals the normal connection in his consciousness is not that of a contract, binding even against one's will, but that of a free association dissoluble at any moment at the will of either.

Thus, in general the marriage situation among the American Poles looks quite hopeless when judged by the standards of the permanent and exclusive conjugal bond. Numerous causes contribute to the progressive dissolution of the monogamous marriage group, and there are no important and general reconstructive factors. Perhaps this process would not constitute a social danger if among the immigrants of peasant origin disorganization of marriage were not as closely connected as it is with demoralization in other fields, and if it did not affect the children as it does. For normal social life may coexist with other forms of family life than those based on the monogamous marriage. But it is obviously impossible for Polish-American society to construct a new type of family organization on some polygamous basis, first because this society is not sufficiently coherent, secondly because the American social and legal system will not allow an explicitly recognized and socially regulated polygamy. However general polygamous arrangements among American Poles may in fact become, they must always bear the outward character of clandestine adultery and thus not only be officially marked as signs of general immorality but must actually contribute to general immorality, i.e., to the decadence of individual life organization. The only possible way to counteract this degeneration of marriage is to give the Polish-American society new ideals of family life or help it develop such ideals. And this can be done only by its actual incorporation into American society, not merely into the American state and economic systems—if American society has really vital family ideals to give.

PART
4

THE DISCOVERY OF
ETHNICITY

This final selection is the first full description of an ethnic community in American history. Thomas and Znaniecki's main point was to convince Americans that the Poles were not simply becoming "American" but were becoming something different and unique: Polish-Americans, with their own culture, values, and institutions. The Poles do not simply "repeat" the culture they shared in Poland, according to Thomas and Znaniecki, but change it so that it becomes serviceable in the American context.

The Polish-American Community

It would seem *a priori* and it is generally assumed that the main problems concerning the immigrants can be stated in terms of individual assimilation or non-assimilation. Since the immigrant is no longer a member of the society from which he came, since he lives in the midst of American society, and since he is connected with it by economic bonds and dependent on its institutions, the only line of evolution left to him seems to be the one leading to a gradual substitution in his consciousness of American cultural values for Polish cultural values and of attitudes adapted to his American environment for the attitudes brought over from the old country. This substitution may be slower or faster and various factors—among others living in racial groups—may influence its pace; but the immigrant (or the immigrant's descendant) is considered as still a Pole in traditions and attitudes, or already an American, or somewhere on the way from Polonism to Americanism, and it is supposed that the essential thing to be studied in relation to him is how he makes this passage.

But, in fact, if we look at the Poles in America not from the standpoint of Polish or American national interests but from that of an objective sociological inquiry, we find that the problem of individual assimilation is at present an entirely secondary and unimportant issue. Of course, there have been many Poles—a few of the first, many more of the second generation—who have become individually absorbed in American society and are now more or less completely assimilated; but the number of such cases in proportion to the total population of Polish origin in this country has been rapidly decreasing in the last fifty years. The fundamental process which has been going on during this period is *the formation of a new Polish-American society* out of those fragments separated from Polish society and embedded in American society. This Polish-American

---

5:x–xiii, 27–93 *passim.* I have omitted the worthwhile discussion of the "Super-Territorial Organization of Polish-American Society"—ed.

society as a whole is, indeed, slowly evolving from Polonism to Americanism, as is shown by the fact that its members, particularly those of the second generation, are continually acquiring more American attitudes and being more influenced by American civilization. But this "assimilation" is not an individual but a group phenomenon, to be compared with such processes as the progressive Germanization of Czech society up to a hundred years ago or the adoption of French culture by the Polish, Russian, and German aristocracies in the course of the eighteenth century. Here the individual does not stand isolated in the midst of a culturally different group. He is part of a homogeneous group in contact with a civilization which influences in various degrees all of the members. And the striking phenomenon, the central object of our investigation, is the formation of this coherent group out of originally incoherent elements, the creation of a society which in structure and prevalent attitudes is neither Polish nor American but constitutes a specific new product whose raw materials have been partly drawn from Polish traditions, partly from the new conditions in which the immigrants live, and partly from American social values as the immigrant sees and interprets them. It is this Polish-American society, not American society, that constitutes the social milieu into which the immigrant who comes from Poland becomes incorporated and to whose standards and institutions he must adapt himself.

Such an evolution has evidently been socially unavoidable. The individual immigrant brings with him to this country his old traditions and attitudes, but of course not the social organization of the old country. He has a tendency to associate with people coming from the same milieu, and as soon as a group of them is agglomerated the old institutions begin spontaneously to reappear. But it is clear that they cannot be revived here with their full original content and significance. First of all, their reconstruction, being the outcome of an unreflective demand for old social values rather than the realization of a conscious plan to have the old system rebuilt, is a relatively slow process. But although the great majority of immigrants is of peasant origin and therefore very conservative, yet their original attitudes necessarily change in the new conditions with time and the demand for the old values grows less insistent and less definite. Secondly, the groups which the immigrants form here are evidently less coherent than the communities in Europe;

around a nucleus of permanent settlers, which is usually of quite recent origin (in a few cases only reaching back to the third generation), there is a shifting mass continually recruited from outsiders who either leave after a short period or are, at least for several years, ready to leave at short notice. Moreover, whereas the old peasant or small town community was in a large measure self-sufficient, most of the needs of its members being satisfied within the group, the Polish-American community depends on the outside world in such a fundamental matter as economic subsistence, draws its income from work in American shops and factories, and consumes almost exclusively American products. For all these reasons, though the steady influx of new immigrants coming directly from Poland and full of old country memories prevents the interest in traditional institutions from disappearing entirely, the social organization which develops spontaneously here is necessarily only a very imperfect imitation of the old Polish original. It still centers around the family and the primary community, and the fundamental principles of direct personal solidarity and conformity with social opinion are still recognized; but of the many varied and coherent beliefs and customs which made these institutions so rich and vital most are either entirely forgotten or inefficient, or even ridiculous, and whatever new beliefs and customary forms of behavior may have developed in, the new conditions are not sufficiently general, numerous, stable, or binding to take adequately the place of the obliterated tradition.

THE BOARDINGHOUSE AND THE JOB

The process by which Polish colonies appear and grow can be observed in detail during the last twenty or thirty years. . . . When a Polish immigrant finds work which pays well and promises to be permanent in a locality where there is no Polish settlement yet, he usually tries at once to attract his friends and relatives from other Polish-American communities. His motives are evident. He has been accustomed to such social response and recognition as only a primary group with old social bonds and uniform attitudes can give, and however well he may be adapted to American economic and political conditions he seldom is at once accepted as a member by an American primary group (or by a primary group of some

other immigrant people). Even if he were he would miss the direct-
ness and warmth of social relations to which he has been accustomed in his own group. Sometimes, indeed, he does not succeed
in attracting anyone. Then if he does not leave the place driven by
loneliness, he becomes gradually absorbed in the American milieu.
Usually, however, a small group of Polish workmen is soon formed;
and their first attempt, partly for economic, partly for social reasons,
is to have a Polish boardinghouse. Often some one of them who
has some money and a wife in America assumes the initiative, brings
his wife as soon as his situation seems settled, rents a large apartment, and takes the others as roomers or boarders. It may happen
that a bachelor marries some Polish girl he knows, with the understanding that they are going to keep a boarding place. Sometimes
under such conditions a wife or a fiancée is even brought from
Europe. Frequently, however, the initiative comes not from an individual but from the group; all the workmen put some money into
renting and furnishing the apartment and induce one of their
number who has a wife or fiancée to bring her. In this case they buy
their own food and the woman only cooks it and cleans the house,
receiving for the services a small sum from each ($1 to $2 a week)
and by tacit understanding feeding herself and her children on her
boarders' superfluous food.

If the locality has a permanent industry, the small Polish colony
continues to grow, partly by invited, partly by independent arrivals.
Almost every individual or small family once settled attracts new
members from the outside, however large the colony may already
be, provided the economic conditions are favorable. The reason
why, even when there is a Polish group formed, its members still
invite their friends and relatives to come is once more to be found
in the desire for response and the desire for recognition. As long
as the Polish immigrant is isolated among Americans or immigrants
of different nationalities, he welcomes the arrival of any Pole.

THE FAMILY SYSTEM

The influx of new immigrants often becomes for a time the most
important factor in [a community's] growth. Later when the community is definitely settled marriages and births—at first relatively
insignificant—gradually acquire the predominant importance.

In this respect it must be remembered that from the standpoint of the traditional family system the family group should tend to be as numerous as possible and that this old conception perfectly harmonizes with the view of the Catholic Church, according to which many children are to be considered a "blessing of God." Of course the family system loses much of its power through emigration, but it remains still strong enough, at least in the first generation, to prevent any rapid decay of this attitude, which is one of the oldest and most deeply rooted family attitudes. We may add that the immigrant seldom knows any means of preventing childbearing except abortion[1] which is considered shameful—probably because resorted to mostly by unmarried girls—and sexual abstinence, which the peasant considers hardly worthwhile merely in order to limit his family. Moreover, the economic conditions here favor the growth of large families. For although the children cannot be utilized economically as early as they are on a peasant farm in Poland, still there is seldom any real difficulty in bringing them up, for the average wages of an immigrant are certainly sufficient to support a large family on the scale to which he has been accustomed in the old country, if not on a higher one. When the children grow up, they are expected to preserve family solidarity at least to the extent of turning over to the family most of their earnings, so that whatever expenses the family incurs to support them until working age are treated as an investment of the family funds from which a return is expected. Furthermore, a large family is considered normal, for the social and economic status of the second generation will probably be above that of the first here, whereas in the old country a too numerous family often means a division of the property into such small parts that the children are unable to maintain the economic and social level of their parents. And if we realize that the power of the parish is here, as we shall see presently, greater than in Poland and that the parish favors for obvious reasons a rapid growth of the population, it will not be surprising that social opinion maintains the old standard of "propagation" and the prestige of a family group grows with the number of its children. Of course, in cases of individual disorganization all these factors may cease to work. Generally, however, they work well enough to make the Pol-

1. This point is probably incorrect—ed.

ish immigrants at least as prolific as the peasants in the old country. Propagation has been even emphasized recently as a patriotic duty to both Poland and the local colony.

THE MUTUAL BENEFIT SOCIETY

Along with the growth of the new colony goes progress in unity and cohesion. In the beginning the group of Polish immigrants is naturally more or less scattered territorially, particularly when the locality has several factories or mines, since every workman tends to live near his working place. There are no interests to keep it together, except the personal ties of relationship and friendship between particular members of marriage groups and the general feeling of racial solidarity. But individuals always appear in every group—usually those who have had some experience in other Polish-American colonies—with whom the feeling of racial solidarity and perhaps also the desire to play a public role become motives for starting a closer organization. A "society" is established invariably whenever the colony reaches 100 to 300 members. . . .

The first purpose for which such a society is usually established is mutual help in emergencies (sickness, death, and, more seldom, lack of work). For however vague the bond of racial solidarity between the members of a new colony may be originally, it never fails to manifest itself at the death of a member. Usually a severe sickness or disabling accident also provokes sympathetic feelings and the desire to help. Just as in matters concerning the increase of the family, so in cases calling for communal solidarity there are in the conditions surrounding the new Polish-American colony factors that are able to counterbalance in some measure and for a certain time the disorganizing influences of the new milieu. The workman who has no productive property and is hired by the week is evidently more seriously affected by misfortune than the peasant farmer or even the manor servant hired by the year. Yet during times of prosperity his increased earning power makes him more able to help others in case of need and more willing to do so, since money has less value for him than in the old country, particularly after he has once resigned himself to considering his earnings as a means to live rather than as a means to acquire property. Further, the group of workmen constituting a Polish-American colony is isolated and cut off from all wider social milieus, instead of constituting, like a group of working men in Poland, an integral part of a larger society disposing of some wealth. Private charity from wealthy people, which in the country districts of Poland still remains a valuable source of help in emergencies, is thus necessarily very limited in this country. As to public charity, an appeal to a charitable institution is considered even in Poland a mark of social downfall; it is even more of a disgrace in the eyes of Polish immigrants here because of the feeling of group responsibility which is imposed, or thought to be imposed by the American milieu. . . .

Originally, during the early stages in the evolution of a Polish-American community mutual help is exercised sporadically, from case to case, by means of collections made for the benefit of the individual or family in distress. Naturally, the more settled and well-to-do members of the community on whom most of the burden falls are eager to substitute for this unregulated voluntary assistance a regular system of mutual death and sickness insurance and thus favor the establishment of an association which will diminish their risks. The very fact that such a regulation of mutual assistance is necessary shows, of course, that the old naive and unreflective communal solidarity, where each individual had rightful claims on the help of every other individual in a degree dependent on the closeness of their social connection, has been radically modified. As a matter of fact, most of the individuals who under the old system would be the first to be called to assist a member—his nearest relatives and old neighbors—are not here; their function has to be assumed, at least in part, vicariously by relative strangers who in Poland would never be asked to interfere. In the eyes of these, the help which they have to give appears not as a natural duty to be unreflectively performed but as, we might say, an artificial duty, the result of abnormal conditions. And this attitude communicates itself gradually even to those who under the old system would always be obliged to help, as friends and close relatives. The duty to help cannot be disclaimed entirely, for the member in distress is at least a fellow countryman, but it is no longer connected with the very foundation of social life. Mutual insurance is a reflective solution of this difficulty. It is the best method of escaping the conflict between the rudiments of the old attitudes of communal solidarity, strengthened by the feeling of group responsibility, and the individualistic unwillingness to endorse claims for assistance which no longer seem rooted in the very nature of things. Since communal solidarity was a universal social institution among Polish peasants and the new individualistic attitude develops in all immigrant colonies, it is clear that the institution of mutual insurance, being the effect of this combined cause—preexisting institution and new social attitude—must be found everywhere in Polish-American society.

THE PARISH

The society founded in a new colony is much more than a mutual insurance institution. Not only does it bring the scattered members of the colony periodically together, thus actively encouraging social intercourse, but it becomes the social organ of the community, the source of all initiative, and the instrument for the realization of all plans initiated. This is probably the most important of its functions. In a peasant village there is no need of such an organ, for the territorial concentration and the close social cohesion of the village make direct individual initiative and immediate spontaneous cooperation of the concrete group possible from case to case. For the old country community, the *okolica* which includes a number of villages, the ready institutions of the commune, and, in certain matters, the parish are more than sufficient to effect such changes as the community is legally entitled and practically able to introduce into the traditional system. Thus the cooperative organization which in Poland corresponds to the Polish-American society, though it may exercise a strong influence over the primary community in which it exists and works, seldom acts as the organ of this community in proposing or realizing plans concerning the community as a whole except, of course, in its own special line of interest— establishment of cooperative shops for public use, public artistic performances, etc. The Polish-American community, on the contrary, is too loose socially and territorially to do without an organ and has no old political or religious centers which could play this role, while it needs organized initiative much more than the old Polish community whose activities can run for a long time more or less smoothly in the established channels of the traditional system.

Thus, in a new Polish-American colony it is the society which assumes the care of the hedonistic interests of the group by organizing balls, picnics, etc.; of its intellectual interests by giving theatrical representations, inviting lecturers, subscribing to periodicals; of its religious interests by arranging religious services to which some priest from an older Polish colony is invited. It is a center of information for newcomers, visitors, travelers; it sends to the press news about any opportunities which the locality may offer to Poles. It acts as a representative of the colony in its relations with the central institutions of Polish-American society and eventually also with American institutions which try to reach the Polish community for political or social purposes. Thus all the campaigns for funds for Poland and for American Liberty Loans were waged in small communities by these associations. Finally, the great work of the society, through which it assures the permanence of the social cohesion of the colony and gains extraordinary prestige and security, though at the same time resigning its exclusive leadership, is the foundation of a parish.

When studying this important Polish-American institution we should again be careful not to ascribe too much significance to its external form and official purpose. Just as the benefit society is much more than a mutual insurance company, so the Polish-American parish is much more than a religious association for common worship under the leadership of a priest. The unique power of the parish in Polish-American life, much greater than in even the most conservative peasant communities in Poland, cannot be explained by the predominance of religious interests which, like all other traditional social attitudes, are weakened by emigration, though they seem to be the last to disappear completely. The parish is, indeed, simply the old primary community, reorganized and concentrated. In its concrete totality it is a substitute for both the narrower but more coherent village group and the wider but more diffuse and vaguely outlined *okolica*. In its institutional organization it performs the functions which in Poland are fulfilled by both the parish and the commune. It does not control the life of its members as efficiently as did the old community, for, first of all, it seldom covers a given territory entirely and is unable to compel everyone living within this territory to belong to it; secondly, its stock of socially recognized rules and forms of behavior is much poorer; thirdly, the attitudes of its members evolve too rapidly in the new conditions; and finally, it has no backing for its coercive measures in the wider society of which it is a part. But its activities are much broader and more complex than those of a parish or of a commune in the old country.

THE COMMUNITY CENTER

It is a mistake to suppose that a community center established by American social agencies can in its present form even approximately fulfill the social function of a Polish parish. It is an institution imposed from the outside instead of being freely developed by the initiative and cooperation of the people themselves, and this, in addition to its racially unfamiliar character, would be enough to prevent it from exercising any deep social influence. Its managers usually know little or nothing of the traditions, attitudes, and native language of the people with whom they have to deal and therefore cannot become genuine social leaders under any conditions. The institution is based on the type of a club, which is entirely unknown to the Polish peasant. Whatever common activities it tries to develop are always exclusively leisure time activities; and, while these undoubtedly do correspond to a real social need, they are not sufficient by themselves to keep a community together and should be treated only as a desirable superstructure to be raised upon a strong foundation of *economic* cooperation. Whatever real assistance the American social center gives to the immigrant community is the result of the case method, which consists in dealing directly and separately with individuals or families. While this method may bring efficient temporary help to the individual, it does not contribute to the social progress of the community nor does it possess much preventive influence in struggling against social disorganization. Both these purposes can be attained only by organizing and encouraging social self-help on the cooperative basis. Finally, in their relations with immigrants the American social workers usually assume, consciously or not, the attitude of a kindly and protective superiority, occasionally, though seldom, verging on despotism. This attitude may be accepted by peasants fresh from the old country where they have been accustomed to it in their relations with the higher classes, but it is apt to provoke indignation in those who, after a longer stay in this country, have acquired a high racial and personal self-consciousness. In either case the result is the same.

The immigrant associates his connections with the American institution with humiliation, submitted to willing or unwillingly, whereas in his own Polish institutions not only his self-consciousness is respected, but he expects and easily obtains personal recognition. Of course, his priest has also a strong attitude of superiority, but this is fully justified in the peasant's eyes by his sacral character.

THE DEVELOPMENT OF THE COMMUNITY

When the parish has been organized, the mutual help association to which this organization is due ceases to be, of course, the central and only representative institution of the community, for the leadership naturally passes into the hands of the priest. But it does not surrender entirely any of its social functions; it simply shares the initiative in communal matters and the representation of the community with the priest on the one hand, and, on the other hand, with the other associations which now begin to appear in rapid succession. The establishment of the parish opens new fields of social activity, widens the sphere of interests, and calls for more and better social cooperation. For *the ideal of the development of the community,* which did not consciously exist while the community had no organ and was only vaguely conceived and intermittently realized during the period when the local mutual help society played the leading role, becomes now clearly formulated as the common ideal of the whole group and relentlessly pursued. The existence of a framework for the permanent organization of the community in the form of a parish produces both a tendency to utilize this framework to the full extent of its possibilities and a corresponding desire to see the community grow in numbers, wealth, cohesion, and complexity of activities. While individualistic motives—economic reasons with those whose living depends on the Polish colony, desire for wider recognition with those who fulfill public functions, etc.—may give a strong additional incentive to individual activities tending to realize this ideal, the chief foundation of the latter is social. It is the same community spirit that makes the individual identify his interests with those of his group in "we"-feeling, which makes the mass of the population of a state desire its expansion. We shall see the fundamental part which this aspiration to have one's group grow plays in the development of all Polish-American institutions.

The priest, far from limiting the activities of local associations, favors their development and utilizes them consistently as instruments for all purposes connected with the progress of the parish. While in Polish country parishes the chief method of obtaining the cooperation of the community in matters connected with the church is an appeal to the large mass of parishioners directly or through the parish council, in Polish cities the help of religious fraternities is largely used for such purposes as special religious celebrations and pilgrimages, aesthetic improvements of the church building, development of church music and song, organization of charities, etc. In America this system of collaboration of organized groups is extended in two ways. First, in addition to religious fraternities, which are for the most part initiated by the priest himself for purely devotional purposes and remain under his complete control, lay associations with economic or cultural purposes, and more or less independent of the priest, are also expected to contribute to the aims of the parish. Secondly, these aims are no longer limited to matters of cult and charity, but embrace all fields of social life.

THE PAROCHIAL SCHOOL

Immediately after the completion of the church or even before, the parish school is organized. Usually the church is planned as a two-story building, the lower story including class rooms and halls for small meetings. Sometimes a private house is rented or bought for school purposes. Both arrangements prove only provisional usually, for the growth of the parish sooner or later forces it to erect a special school building. There are many parishes—five in Chicago alone—whose school is attended by more than 2,000 children. The teachers are mainly nuns of the various teaching orders, though sometimes priests and lay men-teachers are also found, particularly in the larger colonies. Polish and English are both employed as teaching languages, the proportion varying in different schools.

We cannot study here the much discussed question of the educational inferiority or superiority of parochial schools as compared with public schools. Good or bad, the parochial school is a social product of the immigrant group and satisfies important needs of the latter. The most essential point is neither the religious character of the parochial school, nor even the fact that it serves to preserve in the young generation the language and cultural traditions of the old country; it is the function of the parochial school as a factor of the social unity of the immigrant colony and of its continuity through successive generations. The school is a new, concrete, institutional bond between the immigrants. Its first effect is to bring them together territorially, for it has been noticed that proximity to the school—where the children must go every day—is considered even more desirable than proximity to the church. Further, the education of the children is an interest common to all members, just as the religious interest, and this community is fostered by the participation of the parents in all school celebrations and festivities. But even more important than this unification of the old generation is the bond which the parish school creates between the old and the young generation. Whereas children who go to public school become completely estranged from their parents, if these are immigrants, the parish school, in spite of the fact that its program of studies is in many respects similar to that of the public school, in a large measure prevents this estrangement, not only because it makes the children acquainted with their parents' religion, language, and national history but also because it inculcates respect for these traditional values and for the nation from which they came. Moreover, the school is not only a common bond between all the members of the old generation but is also considered by the young generation as their own institution, thus fostering their interest in the affairs of the Polish-American colony. The parochial school is a necessary expression of the tendency of the immigrant community to self-preservation and self-development.

CONCLUSION

The nationalistic Polish tendencies of the local associations have thus not a political but a racial significance. Their aim is to preserve the cultural stock brought by the immigrants to this country—language, mores, customs, and historical traditions—so as to maintain the racial solidarity of the Poles as an ethnic group, independent of their political allegiance and of any economic, social, or political bonds which may connect each of them individually with their American milieu. The local group does not pretend to cut its members off from their wider social environment or to concentrate all their interests within any territorially limited Polish colony. On the contrary, it seems to endorse in the form of social recognition any activities by which its members participate in American economic, political, or intellectual life and seems proud of whatever recognition they may obtain in American circles. But it presupposes that each member personally appreciates most and is most dependent upon the recognition he gets from his Polish milieu, and particularly that he desires social *response* exclusively from Poles. He is never permitted to put into his relations with Americans the same warmth and immediacy of social feelings as in his relations with Poles; the former are expected to be entirely *impersonal* and institutional (if we may use this term), whereas all purely personal contacts must be limited to his own *gens*. This distinction can be best expressed by saying that the only primary group connections a Pole is supposed to maintain are those which his racial group offers, whereas his relations with racially different social elements must belong exclusively to the secondary group type. The psychology is similar to that of a family or an old village community in contact with modern and more complex forms of social organization; a member of such a primary group may be active outside of it as much as he wishes, may be a link of numerous economic, political, and cultural relations of which the primary group knows little and in which it does not participate, but all the while he is supposed to remain essentially, as a concrete person, a member of this primary group and no other, and whatever he does outside of it he is meant to do *as* member of this family or this community, not as isolated personality. In the same way the American Pole is permitted to take whatever part he desires in American life provided he does it *as a Pole,* and the only forms of participation which are socially condemned are those which tend to incorporate him into American primary groups and to draw him away from his Polish *gens*—that is, marriage, personal friendship, and all kinds of intercourse implying direct personal solidarity.

The local group is the institution whose function with reference to its members consists precisely in strengthening this type of racial solidarity against possible disorganization in a racially different milieu. The association gives the individual in ready form opportunities to satisfy both his desire for recognition and his desire for response. It is small enough to permit every individual to know every other individual, to be interested in the affairs of others, and to provoke their interest in his own affairs. It is large enough to make the individual feel its recognition or lack of recognition as an important matter. It is sufficiently solidary for its opinion to have unity and weight, and at the same time sufficiently loose not to be oppressive, not to provoke any violent revolt.

In accordance with its function its main internal activities are those which from the standpoint of purely objective results would seem either subordinate to other aims or simply incidental—formal meetings and social entertainments. The significance of the formal meeting is not in any way exhausted by the affairs which the group discusses and settles. With regard to its psychological effects its most important part is the actual, direct social connection which is established between the members by the very fact of their being together and discussing.

EPILOGUE

Eli Zaretsky

From the work of the past generation of social historians, we can supplement and to some extent correct Thomas and Znaniecki by reconstructing the place of the immigrants in shaping the industrial working class. The first point to understand is the significance of the family economy—the fact that family members pooled their resources. This was the practice in Poland, where the typical rural family owned a marginal plot of land that produced an income that had to be supplemented by wages obtained elsewhere. Since the average peasant holding was shrinking, the danger was that the family would lose its land. The wage for unskilled labor was eight times greater in the United States than in Poland, and the first Polish immigrants, known as *za chlebem* ("for bread"), aimed to help their families hold on to their land.[1]

Eighty percent of the Polish immigrants worked as unskilled laborers in the expanding mass production industries: iron and steel mills, machine shops and piers, packinghouses, textile mills, and coal mines. The most unstable concentrations of industrial labor were those in mining towns, on ships, or in logging camps, where one found large numbers of single men.[2] In the new industrial enterprises the Polish immigrants encountered a small, native-born, older, skilled working class—frequently English, Irish, or German in origin—with a strong sense of itself. In the nineteenth-century factory, skilled workers had a great deal of control over the process of production. They often owned their own tools, took great pride in their craft, and had a powerful sense of their rights. Through hard work, savings, and familial cooperation they had frequently acquired homes and were active, respected members of the community who could call on the support of nonworkers in the event of a strike.[3] By contrast, the Polish immigrants were among the early vassals of machine production with no control over the conditions, character, or product of their own labor. Because their orientation was to Poland, they preferred to live in boardinghouses with a hired housekeeper and work the longest possible hours in order to save as much money as they could.

Between 1880 and 1920, as America's basic industrial structure took shape, the division between native-born and immigrant became less important. In 1892, when the Carnegie Steel plant in Homestead tried to destroy the steel union, three thousand mostly immigrant, nonunionized, unskilled workers supported the union. Despite the Homestead strike's defeat, union organizers in coal, steel, and meatpacking drives—the three industries in which an effort to organize industrywide unions was made before the 1930s—learned to speak and write the immigrants' languages, respect their customs, and encourage leadership from within the immigrants' ranks. In the Pennsylvania anthracite field, unionization only succeeded when the tightly knit, communal settlements of East Europeans were able to mobilize public opinion and enforce discipline on the strikers.[4] At the Jones and Laughlin steel mill in Pittsburgh, Poles dominated the hammer shop, Germans, the carpentry shop, and Serbs, the blooming mill, but each group shared with native-born workers a common set of working-class values. According to David Montgomery, "the impulse of peasant immigrants to work furiously when an authority figure was present and loaf in his absence (a tendency that persisted strongly in steel mills) was soon exchanged in coal mines or car shops for the craftsman's ethic of refusing to work while the boss was watching."[5]

Eventually about two-thirds of the Polish immigrants ended up staying in the United States. As women began to emigrate from Poland, a Polish-American working-class family and community life developed in America. In Chicago's Packingtown, where a different ethnic group could be found on every block, the entire community supported the Amalgamated Meatcutters when, in 1904, it launched a drive for a minimum wage for unskilled labor. After the drive, the rate of home buying rose, the crime rate declined, and fewer people repatriated. Contacts among different ethnic groups took place in the streets (where people fled to avoid the congested tenements), in the casual labor agencies, and in the saloons that were centers for weddings, dances, fraternal lodges, and political meetings for every ethnic group. The union drive of 1918 was supported by every community organization. After a temporary victory, neighborhood park benches were named "eight-hour benches" because, for the first time, men had time to spend with their families.[6]

The Polish peasant's family economy was recreated in the American working class. "That word ['job'] came into my vocabulary in 1894," wrote settlement house worker Mary MacDowell in 1928, "and has since become almost a sacred word. . . . It is the word first learned by the immigrant, the children lisp it, and the aged cling to it to the end: . . . 'please get me a job.'"[7] The reason is clear. Between 1877 and 1910 the wage for unskilled laborers in the United States was $10 or $11 per week, while the minimum income required to support a family was estimated at $15, which did not include weddings, accidents, sicknesses, and funerals, in a time when there was no governmental social insurance.[8]

As a result, immigrants moved to areas that combined male and female employment (for example, coal mines and textile mills) and sought work for women at home: stringing and wiring tags, assembling valentines, sewing rags into carpets, covering baseballs, pressing seams, taping underwear, and taking in laundry and, especially, boarders.[9] The same considerations determined at what age children would enter the mills and how much of their pay they would give to their families. And the same need to pool incomes fostered a drive toward homeownership among the Poles, who rented out the best units and lived in the worst (frequently the attics) themselves. Homeownership facilitated boarding and offered a hedge against aging, which began early for unskilled laborers. When World War I cut off the flow of boarders, married women were forced to seek work in the plants. A 1918 study showed that these women, most with children, rarely slept more than a couple of hours a night and on laundry days did not sleep at all. When Judge Samuel Alschuler visited Polish workers' homes during the 1918 strike, he found children as young as six caring for infants, cabbage and stale bread the only food, and a government placard in the window admonishing "Don't waste food."[10]

The period in which *The Polish Peasant* was being published— 1918–20—was also a period in which the mass organizing drives of the early twentieth century were defeated. An ethnic middle class with a strong commitment to "American values" emerged. Flag Day parades, stock-buying drives, and anti-Bolshevist Americanization leaflets in the immigrants' language were joined to "Buy Polish"

campaigns. Most Poles, however, remained in the industrial working class. During the twenties, a conservative, family- and commu-
nity-centered working-class culture developed. According to one
historian: "Many children viewed their immigrant fathers as, above
all else, hard workers. If sons had any image of their father, it included manual work as an inevitable aspect of life. Indeed, the fathers served as 'models of immobility.' A Polish-American described
his parents as individuals who believed in 'work, work, work, and
work.' . . . They were tireless and always feared the loss of their jobs
since they had nothing to fall back on."[11] On the other hand, the
possibility for militant action on the part of the Poles, especially
given changes in the political climate and the government, became
clear in the 1930s. Much of the subsequent history of the Polish-
American community would depend on their relations to other
groups, especially African Americans, as well as to the emancipation of women. These were questions barely touched on by Thomas and Znaniecki and only now being studied by social historians.

NOTES

1. Victor Greene, "The Poles," in *Harvard Encyclopedia of American Ethnic Groups* (Cambridge: Harvard University Press, 1981), pp. 798–99.

2. Clark Kerr and A. J. Siegel, "The Interindustry Propensity to Strike—
An International Comparison" in *Labor and Management in Industrial Soci-
ety*, ed. Clark Kerr (New York: Doubleday, 1964). See also *Workers in the
Industrial Revolution*, ed. Peter N. Stearns and Daniel J. Walkowitz (New
Brunswick, N.J.: Transaction, 1974).

3. David Montgomery, *Workers' Control in America: Studies in the History
of Work, Technology and Labor Struggles* (New York: Cambridge University
Press, 1979), pp. 13–14.

4. Peter Roberts commented: "When they organize they move with an
unanimity that is seldom seen" (*Anthracite Coal Industry* [New York: Mac-
millan, 1901], p. 172).

5. Montgomery, *Workers' Control*, pp. 42–43. See David Montgomery, *The
Fall of the House of Labor* (New York: Cambridge University Press, 1987); John
Bodnar, *Workers' World: Kinship, Community, and Protest in Industrial Society,
1900–1940* (Baltimore: Johns Hopkins University Press, 1982); Bodnar, "Im-
migration and Modernization: The Case of Slavic Peasants in Industrial
America," *Journal of Social History* 10 (Fall 1976): 44–67; Bodnar, Michael
Weber, and Roger Simon, "Migration, Kinship, and Urban Adjustment:
Blacks and Poles in Pittsburgh, 1900–1930," *Journal of American History* 66

(1977): 548–65; Tamara Hareven, "The Laborers of Manchester, New Hampshire, 1912–1922," *Labor History* 16 (1975): 249–65; Bodnar, Roger Simon, and Michael P. Weber, *Lives of Their Own: Blacks, Italians, and Poles in Pittsburgh, 1900–1960* (Urbana: University of Illinois Press, 1982).

6. See James R. Barrett, *Work and Community in the Jungle: Chicago's Packinghouse Workers, 1894–1922* (Urbana: University of Illinois Press, 1987).

7. Howard Wilson, *Mary MacDowell, Neighbor* (Chicago: University of Chicago Press, 1928), pp. 69–70.

8. Barrett, *Work and Community in the Jungle;* Andrea Graziosi, "Common Laborers, Unskilled Workers, 1850–1915," *Labor History* 22 (Fall 1981): 518.

9. Caroline Golab, "The Impact of the Industrial Experience on the Immigrant Family: The Huddled Masses Reconsidered," in *Immigrants in Industrial America, 1850–1920,* ed Richard L. Ehrlich (Charlottesville: University Press of Virginia, 1977), pp. ix–x, 19–25.

10. Barrett, *Work and Community in the Jungle.*

11. Bodnar, "Immigration and Modernization," 56–57; Bodnar, Weber, and Simon, "Migration, Kinship, and Urban Adjustment." For a truly bleak portrait of the second-generation Polish-American family, see Arnold Green "The 'Cult of Personality' and Sexual Relations," *Psychiatry* 4 (1941), and "The Middle Class Male Child and Neurosis," *American Sociological Review* 2 (Feb. 1946): 2.

WILLIAM I. THOMAS was born in 1863, in Russell County, Virginia, the son of a man who combined preaching and farming. He received a Ph.D. in English literature from the University of Tennessee in 1886 and in 1888–89 studied folk psychology at Göttingen and Berlin. Between 1890 and 1895 he taught English at Oberlin College. While on leave in 1893–94, he entered the University of Chicago to study under the direction of Albion Small and Charles Henderson. Considered one of the discipline's founders, Thomas taught sociology at Chicago from 1895 to 1918. Following his first book, *Sex and Society* (1907), he was put in charge of the Helen Culver Fund for Race Psychology, under whose auspices he recruited Florian Znaniecki and produced *The Polish Peasant in Europe and America*. Between 1918 and his death in 1947, Thomas held a succession of research grants, foundation appointments, and temporary lectureships at a series of universities, including Harvard, the New School for Social Research, and the University of Stockholm. His other works include *Source Book for Social Origins* (1909), *Old World Traits Transplanted*, with Robert E. Park and Herbert Miller (1921), *The Unadjusted Girl* (1923), and *Primitive Behavior* (1937).

FLORIAN WITOLD ZNANIECKI was born in 1882, in Świątniki, Poland, the son of an estate manager. His earliest instruction, at the hands of tutors, emphasized languages, and in 1903 he published *Cheops: A Poem of Fantasy*. Due to underground activity as a Polish nationalist at the University of Warsaw, Znaniecki never received a baccalaureate degree. He traveled and studied in Switzerland, France, and Italy and received his Ph.D. in philosophy from the University of Krakow in 1909. Ineligible for an academic post for political reasons, Znaniecki became director of the Emigrant's Protective Association and it was in this capacity that he met Thomas in 1913. In 1920 he became professor of sociology at the University of Poznan, where he founded the Polish Sociological Institute and the *Polish Sociological Review*. From 1940 until his death in 1958, he was professor of sociology at the University of Illinois. His other writings include *Cultural Reality* (1919), *The Laws of Social Psychology* (1925), *The Method of Sociology* (1934), *Social Actions* (1936), *The Social Role of the Man of Knowledge* (1940), and *Cultural Sciences* (1952).

ELI ZARETSKY is a graduate of the University of Michigan and received his Ph.D. in American history from the University of Maryland in 1978. The author of *Capitalism, the Family, and Personal Life* (1976), *Psychoanalysis: From the Psychology of Authority to the Politics of Identity* (1996), and numerous articles in social theory and in history, he is an associate professor of history at the University of Missouri, Columbia.

UNIVERSITY OF ILLINOIS PRESS
1325 SOUTH OAK STREET
CHAMPAIGN, ILLINOIS 61820-6903
WWW.PRESS.UILLINOIS.EDU